THE
DECLINE OF LIBERALISM
AS AN IDEOLOGY

WITH PARTICULAR REFERENCE TO
GERMAN POLITICO-LEGAL THOUGHT

BY

JOHN H. HALLOWELL

HOWARD FERTIG

NEW YORK · 1971

First published in 1943 as Volume 1, No. 1,
University of California Publications in Political Science

HOWARD FERTIG, INC. EDITION ·1971
Published by permission of the Regents of the University of California.

Library of Congress Catalog Card Number: 75-80554

PRINTED IN THE UNITED STATES OF AMERICA
BY NOBLE OFFSET PRINTERS, INC.

PATRI DILECTO
FILIUS GRATUS

What the notions of "form" and "harmony" were to Plato, that the notions of "individuality" and "competition" were to the nineteenth century. God had placed his bow in the skies as a symbol; and the strip of colours, rightly read, spelt "competition." The prize to be competed for was "life." Unsuccessful competitors died; and thus, by a beautiful provision of nature, ceased from constituting a social problem.

—A. N. WHITEHEAD, *Adventures of Ideas.*

PREFACE

WITH THE RISE to power of the National Socialists in Germany liberal political institutions collapsed like a house of cards tumbled over by a gust of wind. The rapidity and completeness with which liberal institutions were destroyed suggested that the spirit in which these institutions were originally conceived had reached a heretofore unsuspected stage of inner degeneracy. For no nation, however severely beaten into submission, however cleverly seduced by the winning wiles of a master propagandist, would calmly submit, without resistance or civil war, to the wanton destruction of political institutions if these were securely and deeply rooted in the spiritual consciousness of the people. That it was possible expeditiously to annihilate liberal institutions without more than a murmur of dissent is eloquent testimony to the degeneracy of German postwar liberalism.

How was it possible for prominent professors, judges, lawyers, and civil servants, who before 1933 were professed liberals, to accept, and some even to acclaim, a despotism that not only repudiates the fundamental postulates of liberalism but seeks actively to banish every liberal institution from the face of the earth? It is the purpose of this study to suggest a possible answer.

In 1837, when a Hanoverian government abrogated a constitution it had sworn to uphold that act met with vigorous popular protest, a protest that found intellectual expression in the now famous statement drafted by seven Goettingen professors. But in 1933 those German intellectuals who did protest against despotism were conspicuous because they were comparatively few. In 1933 there was no Dahlmann to ask, as he did in 1837, "Must I teach henceforward that the supreme principle of the State is that whatever pleases those in power is law? As a man of honor, I would cease to teach rather than sell to my audience for truth that which is a lie and a deceit." That there was no organized collective resistance in 1933 such as there was in 1837 suggests, not that the German intellectual of the twentieth century was any less brave or vocal than the intellectual of a century before, but rather that his liberal convictions were less securely and deeply rooted.

In view of this the suspicion arises that liberalism was not murdered, as is often said, but that it committed suicide. The suspicion arises that probably the death of the liberal ideology in Germany and the subsequent destruction of the institutions which were originally conceived and established to translate its aspirations into practice is to be attributed less to the machinations of Hitler and the National Socialists than to the liberals themselves. A desire to test the validity of this hypothesis motivated the undertaking of this study. And if liberalism, by some inner necessity to be found in the ideology itself, develops from something live and vigorous to something decadent and degenerate then this analysis, although confined for the purposes of this study to Germany, should have especial interest to those who are concerned about the survival of liberal political institutions wherever found.

To ascertain *when* and *how* liberalism as an ideology became decadent in Germany is the purpose of this study. Except by implication I have not tried to answer the somewhat more difficult question *why* liberalism became decadent. Confronted with the formalism of a Kelsen, who, while asserting himself a liberal, in effect declares *every* state to be a *Rechtsstaat,* I have endeavored to search further for the roots of his thought and to examine the development that produced him. The process of formalization that characterizes the decline of the liberal ideology is described in the pages that follow.

Although, for the purposes of this study, attention has been focused primarily upon the development of ideas rather than institutions, I do not feel that my study is unrelated to practical political developments. I recognize a mutual dependence and a reciprocal influence between ideas and institutions, between theory and practice, between ideologies and practical politics. Ideas are not generated in a vacuum. They do have a sociological, as well as a physical, background. In focusing attention primarily upon ideas I attempt to keep this in mind but I am particularly aware that institutions, as the structural expressions of conceptual schemes, need a consistent ideational foundation if they are to enjoy a vigorous and live existence.

Vigorous institutions require deep-rooted convictions. So long as there is a close correlation between the faith, the aspirations and ideals, of any particular society and the institutions that are established to translate those aspirations into practice, the order thereby created appears stable, rational, and orderly. When, however, this close correlation is lacking, when institutions, in the eyes of the great mass of people, fail to fulfill the faith which originally inspired them, the order becomes disorder, the system appears irrational and degenerate. Rationality itself, then, is in large measure a function of the relationship between man's faith and man's deeds, his "inarticulate premises" and his experience, his philosophy of life and his way of life. While I have directed my attention primarily to an analysis of the development of the liberal ideology, I have by implication, I believe, said something of significance about the development of liberal institutions. Political institutions are shaped, to a considerable degree at least, by man's conception of himself and of his place and function in society.

If we recognize that liberalism in the Germany of 1933 was decadent the logical inference is that there must be some liberalism "as it ought to be." The word decadent itself suggests a departure from or perversion of original or integral ideas. If one acknowledges the degeneracy of postwar German liberalism as it found expression in the writings of men like Kelsen and Carl Schmitt (and one is forced to do so if he concedes that irresponsibility is incompatible with individual freedom) he must further concede that there is such a thing as liberalism integrally conceived. The notion of decadence presupposes it.

Accordingly, the first task of my study has been the reconstruction of liberalism as an integral system of ideas, the delineation of the idea of liberalism in the Platonic sense. Since definitions at best are but symbols of a process of thought, I have not endeavored to define liberalism in succinct phrases but rather to distinguish it by describing in some detail the attributes that characterize it. In order to do so it has been necessary to examine the philosophical roots of liberal thought, to find the fundamental presuppositions that constitute its "inarticulate premises."

Thus, so far as my study is accurate, it should contribute something to a more precise conception of liberalism. This is needed today and especially in our own country where practically everyone calls himself a liberal and embodies in the term all that is congenial to his particular way of thinking. It has been customary in this country to distinguish the continental meaning of the word liberal from the American use of the word. Now, although it has been fairly clear that when a contemporary American uses the word liberal he means something very different from the eighteenth-century continental meaning of the word, it has not been clear in a positive way what he actually means by it. This confusion is possibly the result of an uncertain, if not aberrant, conception of liberalism. For the sake of clarity, the word liberal should be used to describe one who believes in liberalism; it should be more precisely defined than it is today or else it should be abandoned.

After describing the fundamental elements of integral liberalism, as found in German thought and elsewhere, I have endeavored to trace, through the works of representative German politico-legal thinkers, the process by which these elements were in part discarded and in part transformed into concepts with different meaning and implication. By tracing the dialectical evolution of fundamental liberal concepts I have tried to ascertain if there is some "law" of development peculiar to liberalism.

This analysis is based largely upon the writings of representative German jurists. Since in Germany it was the jurists more than any others who concerned themselves with the problems and concepts of political thought it is impossible to make any clear and decisive distinction between political and legal thought, even if it were desirable to do so. I have made no pretense at exhaustiveness, but I have tried to select thinkers and writings which appeared to me to be most representative of trends of thought characteristic of the period under examination. The broad general development has interested me more than the details of debates within particular schools of thought, the highway of thought more than the innumerable byways that lead from it.

Throughout I have sketched the development of liberalism with particular attention to its elements as I believe them to be. I have been more interested, therefore, in the changing meaning and evolution of certain fundamental concepts than in the chronological, strictly historical, development of political ideas. The logical development of a concept rarely, if ever, corresponds to its chronological treatment by various writers, and, in order to clarify my analysis, I have abandoned the strictly historical method of examination in favor of a logical method.

To some extent I have sought to correlate the development of liberal political concepts with similar developments in other fields.

Such correlations are necessarily incomplete but are intended only to indicate here and there that tendencies found in political-legal thought are not peculiar to this realm of thought alone. These correlations serve only to indicate that modes of thought found in political-legal philosophy are part of a general intellectual consciousness peculiar to the period and society under examination.

This study should be regarded as an interpretative essay since it makes no pretense to fathom what is an infinitely broad and fathomless subject. If, however, it suggests an interpretation of the development of liberalism which has remained undiscovered or neglected by other writers, it will have justified my efforts.

For their friendly encouragement and constructive criticism I am indebted to Professors William S. Carpenter and Gerhart Niemeyer of Princeton University under whose direction this study was originally begun and submitted as a doctoral dissertation at Princeton. I am particularly indebted to Professor Niemeyer for it was his keen and original insight into the problem and his familiarity with German sources that guided me through a maze of literature and aided me immeasurably in the task of analysis. I owe a special debt of gratitude to my former colleague Professor Malbone W. Graham of the University of California at Los Angeles for a painstaking reading of the manuscript that helped me to avoid many errors of style and of thought.

But it goes without saying that for any errors of fact or of judgment which may be found in the pages that follow I am alone responsible.

JOHN H. HALLOWELL

LOS ANGELES, CALIFORNIA
January 26, 1943

CONTENTS

CHAPTER I

INTEGRAL LIBERALISM AND THE PROCESS OF FORMALIZATION

*... jenseits von Gut und Böse gibt es weder Recht noch
Staat. Nur durch konkrete Rechtsideale wird der kon-
krete Staat legitimiert und wesentlich integriert.*
—HERMANN HELLER

UNDERLYING POSTULATES

LIBERALISM is the product of a climate of opinion that came into existence with the Renaissance and Reformation. It is the political expression of an individualistic *Weltanschauung*. As a political ideology born of a particular historical period in a specific sociological environment it is subject, like all such systems of ideas, to development, decline, and death. Elements of its doctrine may survive its demise as a dominant and consistent ideology but as a system of ideas it is necessarily subject to change with the changes in the mode of thought and the sociological conditions that gave rise to it.

For the ways in which men think about things, like the thoughts themselves, are conditioned, and in part determined, by the historical and sociological environment in which they live. Ideas are not generated in a mental vacuum. They are not drawn out of thin air magician-like by isolated individual minds. On the contrary, as Karl Mannheim has expressed it, every individual "finds himself in an inherited situation with patterns of thought that are appropriate to this situation and attempts to elaborate further the inherited modes of response or to substitute others for them in order to deal more adequately with the new challenges which have arisen out of the shifts and changes in his situation."[1]

Thought, however, involves a great deal more than the mere sensory awareness of one's physical and social environment. Thought is something more than sense perception, something more than a mere mechanical reflex expression of physical stimuli. For the same physical stimulus may produce a variety of responses just as the same kind of response may result from very different

[1] For notes to chap. i, see pp. 125–127.

[1]

kinds of stimuli. The effect of physical stimuli upon individual
action depends very largely upon the context in which they occur
and upon the relative value attached to them by the context and
by the individual.[2]

Thought involves abstraction and conceptualization. The most
detached thinker actually does something more than record "facts."
Indeed, the ascertainment of facts would be impossible without
some conceptual scheme in terms of which facts might be observed
and ordered. The observation of facts requires not only sense
perception but judgments as to value and significance. And even
the scientist, who claims to be the most impersonal observer, necessarily must fit the data made available to him by his senses into
some preformulated conceptual scheme.[3]

To understand the thought of any man, therefore, it is essential
to know with what "freely invented" concepts he starts, to know
the point of view from which he observes and interprets life about
him. It is necessary to know his premises as well as the conclusions
which he draws from these. The things which he presupposes, which
he may regard as self-evident, are as important to an understanding of his thought as are the ideas which he expresses and his
manner of expression. Implicit assumptions, in other words, are
as important as explicit assertions.

What applies to an individual's thinking is applicable as well
to the thought of any particular historical period. As Whitehead
has expressed it: "There will be some fundamental assumptions
which adherents of all the variant systems within the epoch un-
consciously presuppose. Such assumptions appear so obvious that
people do not know what they are assuming because no other way
of putting things has ever occurred to them."[4] We are incapable
of recognizing and analyzing the assumptions of a particular
epoch so long as they provide a satisfactory explanation of our
experience. The fact that men are now engaged in analyzing the
presuppositions underlying our own age, and indeed the fact that
we are conscious of them, is probably evidence that they no longer
provide the satisfactory link with experience which they have to
this moment. That other ways of "putting things" have begun to
occur to us characterizes an age of transition and presages the
decline of a climate of opinion that has nurtured man's intellect
since the Renaissance.

As the presuppositions of an age change so the systems of ideas which are derived (in part) from these change. Liberalism is based upon presuppositions characterizing the individualistic *Weltanschauung;* as these presuppositions are replaced by others, liberalism itself must give way to systems of ideas more congenial to the logic of the new premises. For example, liberalism could not have emerged in the Middle Ages for there existed then no concept of individuality comparable to that of the modern age and liberalism is premised upon this very concept. The logical dependence of liberalism upon certain fundamental premises or assumptions relates its development and existence to the development and existence of these underlying presuppositions.

The existence of liberalism depends also upon certain sociological factors. It is related to these to the extent that modes of thought are related to a way of life. If liberalism is dependent for its existence upon values and modes of thought peculiar to the age of individualism, it is equally dependent upon a specific sociological environment. Liberalism required not only the existence of the concept of an autonomous individual but also an environment congenial to the exercise of individual autonomy. The values posited by liberalism would have been meaningless apart from an environment and institutions in which these values could find practical expression in everyday life.

INDIVIDUALISM AND LIBERALISM

Since liberalism is premised upon the individualistic *Weltanschauung* that emerged in the late fifteenth and sixteenth centuries, it is necessary to give some brief attention to the underlying presuppositions of that perspective. In this way the philosophical foundations of liberalism may be brought into sharper focus.

The period of the Renaissance and Reformation accelerated an intellectual movement that had its roots in the later Middle Ages. Interest in classical literature and civilization was stimulated as men sought to find in antiquity patterns of thought and a way of life applicable to the new situation, which was characterized by the crumbling of the universal Church, the rise of the nation-state, and the disintegration of the feudal economy. The Christian ideas of the Middle Ages were merged with Stoic conceptions of individuality to produce the individualism of modern times.

Reinhold Niebuhr emphasizes the novelty of this conception of individuality. He says:

> If Protestantism represents the final heightening of the idea of individuality within terms of the Christian religion, the Renaissance is the real cradle of that very unchristian concept and reality: the autonomous individual. . . . Ostensibly Renaissance thought is a revival of classicism, the authority of which is either set against the authority of Christianity or used to modify the latter. Yet classic thought has no such passion for the individual as the Renaissance betrays. The fact is that the Renaissance uses an idea which could have grown only upon the soil of Christianity. It transplants this idea to the soil of classic rationalism to produce a new concept of individual autonomy, which is known in neither classicism nor Christianity.[5]

Not only were individuals thought to be equal entities, equal in moral worth by virtue of God-given souls, but also they were thought to possess a reason, divine in origin, that was capable of restraining passion and emotion through the realization of a potential, rational, universal order. Just as the period of the Middle Ages was "an age of faith, based upon reason" so the modern age has been "an age of reason, based upon faith."[6]

The attribution to each individual of an element of "divine reason" made it possible to ascribe a dignity and autonomy of will to every human being in a way that had not been possible in the Middle Ages. From this conception, moreover, there issued others equally important. As Troeltsch observes:

> Several conclusions are directly derived from this assumption. It explains the claim which the individual makes, and the duty which he admits, that Reason should be acknowledged to be the Natural—which is also to say the Divine—Law. Again, it provides the foundation of all human legal institutions, which thus become directly identical, in the last analysis, with moral principles. Finally, it furnishes the ideal of a single organization or society of all mankind.[7]

During the Middle Ages all law was conceived as being of divine origin for then the whole world was thought of as part of a harmonious universe that began and ended with God. Individual will was regarded as incapable of creation and, so far as it was recognized at all, it was conceived as participating in God's work only as an agent. Law was part of the divine plan and in no way dependent upon individual will or consent. The individual was free to sin but free in no other sense. The order of reality was created and influenced by God alone. As a consequence there was no conceivable conflict between the ideal and the real, between the objective and the subjective nor even between real wills—for if a will violated God's law it was no longer within the system, it was an act of sin. As a consequence there was no question of obligation in the modern sense.

But in the sixteenth and seventeenth centuries, as a result of the new concept of individuality, and particularly of the conception of the autonomy of individual will, men were conscious of an antinomy between will and norm, man and nature, what is and what ought to be. Unlike the medieval man who started with the conception of an immutable universal order embodied in God, they were conscious of an individual capable of creation, a man endowed with will and interests. Having turned from revelation to reason, men sought by rational methods to achieve again a harmony that the religious wars of the sixteenth century had failed to attain.

Men sought within the confines of human nature principles from which legal, moral, and economic forms might be deduced. Whereas the medieval man started with the conception of a Divine universal order, modern man started with the conception of individuality, of human nature. As a consequence natural law became separated in the sixteenth century from the authority of God and was based upon human nature. Grotius, for example, defined it as ". . . a dictate of right reason, which points out that an act, according as it is or is not in conformity with rational nature, has in it a quality of moral baseness or moral necessity; and that, in consequence, such an act is either forbidden or enjoined by the author of nature, God."[8] It is not by revelation that one discovers natural law but by human reason.

In short, the concept of individuality which emerged at the close of the Middle Ages emphasized several things: the inherent moral worth and spiritual equality of each individual, the dignity of human personality, the autonomy of individual will, and the essential rationality of men. It ascribed to human beings a creative function which had been denied in the Middle Ages.

In the Middle Ages there was no separation of private and public spheres of activity. There was no state in the modern sense and hence, no distinction between the "state" and "society." Feudalism, as a system of reciprocal rights and duties, was based upon personal, legal relationships, organized hierarchically. The distinction between political authority and personal rights was blurred.

With the disintegration of the feudal order, prerogatives of rulership, which earlier had been thought of as the private property of the ruler, were gradually transferred to the sphere of public administration. By virtue of the peculiar circumstances of the times, political authority necessitated the introduction of general systems of taxation, the creation of bureaucracies, and the employment of standing armies. Thus, gradually, the prerogatives of rulership became impersonalized. And when there was attached to these new phenomena, notably by Machiavelli, the concept of *raison d'état,* the idea of the modern state emerged.

As a consequence of this impersonalization of the political order, the individual acquired a sphere of autonomy such as he never knew in medieval society. This sphere, which now corresponded to "society," was set apart from the impersonal, public, political order which was the "state." The medieval problem of the relationship between ecclesiastical and secular authority was replaced in importance by the problem of the relationship between state and society, between the spheres of political authority and individual autonomy. Liberalism emerged as a specific answer to this problem. It could not have existed apart from these particular conditions. It cannot exist when this problem is no longer vital or meaningful.

THE LOGIC OF LIBERALISM

The essential postulate of integral liberalism is the absolute value and dignity of human personality. Now if individuals are moral entities, equal in value, they can submit to no will that is arbitrary or capricious. To do so would be to deny their moral equality, to deny the dignity which they possess as human beings endowed with reason.

But authority is necessary to social order. How then can the two be reconciled? Liberalism answered that the individual can only submit to an authority that is impersonal, objective, and eternal. He cannot submit to the will of another individual nor to any arbitrary authority. The only authority to which the individual can submit is to the impersonal authority of law.

Integral liberalism, accordingly, does not espouse freedom for the individual from all restraint—that would be license, not freedom. That would not guarantee freedom for every individual but lead inevitably to anarchy and finally to the imposition of the will of the stronger upon the others. On the contrary, liberalism espouses responsible freedom, freedom under the law, for only in this way can the freedom of each be secured.

The content of this law is thought to be discoverable by reason. The limitation which integral liberalism places upon individual will consists of certain eternal truths and values transcending all individuals and discoverable by reason. In the seventeenth and eighteenth centuries these truths were thought to be embodied in a natural law derived from human nature. Positive law was conceived of as at once the product of will and the particular expression of a universal principle. The responsibility for making positive law conform to natural law devolved upon the individual. Individual will fashioned the particular law but its form and content were supposed to be derived from universal principles. One element was dynamic, the other static. Human will was free only within the limits set by values transcending individuals and objectified in natural law. The conception was very largely Platonic for it conceived of individuals giving particular expression to universals.

Integral liberalism bridged the gap between the natural liberty of the individual and the natural law of humankind, between subjective will and objective order, by the sense of obligation. The universal order of the Middle Ages required no individual recognition for its existence but the universal order of the seventeenth century rested entirely upon the individual for its actualization. According to this conception, it is the duty of the individual to carry out the dictates of objective reason, subordinating passion and desire, in order to realize the potential order embodied in reason. The whole obligation for realizing order rests upon the individual, and more specifically upon individual conscience.

Conscience is the keystone of the whole structure. Order is potentially embodied in truths and values transcending all individuals but only dispassionate, objective reason can translate this potential order into actuality. The law is an ideal requiring concrete wills and concrete actions to be realized; it is a form ready to be filled in by individual wills. *Only conscience bids the individual to follow the dictates of reason rather than those of interest. At the basis of*

*this conception of law is conscience (theoretically ethics) and upon
the conscientiousness of individuals rests the choice between order
and anarchy.*

Inherent in the notion of limitation were two theories, as Roscoe
Pound observes: "On the one hand there was a theory of limitations
upon human activities imposed by reason in view of human nature,
on the other hand there was a theory of moral qualities inherent
in human beings, or natural rights, demonstrated by reason as
deductions from human nature."[9] The first theory had been worked
out by predecessors of Grotius in the sixteenth century, derived
in part from Stoic conceptions; the theory of natural rights was
developed, among others of his time, by Grotius. Having accepted
the principle of Roman law that no individual should harm another, that he should give to each person his due, Grotius was faced
with the problem of what constituted injury.

He was forced to answer two questions, as formulated by Pound:
"What is there in personality that makes aggression an injury?
What is it that constitutes anything one's own?"[10] Grotius, and
those who followed him, answered—*natural rights,* "not merely
natural law, as before, not merely principles of eternal validity, but
certain qualities inherent in persons and demonstrated by reason
and recognized by natural law, to which therefore the national law
ought to give effect."[11] This was a new conception, a conception
made possible only by presupposing the existence of individual
entities equal in moral worth by virtue of God-given souls and
endowed with an element of "divine reason."

Rights, as conceived by Grotius and his contemporaries, were
something substantive; they were not simply formal. For a right,
as Grotius defined it, was "that quality in a person which makes
it just or right for him either to possess *certain* things or to do
certain actions."[12] The end of law in the Middle Ages was conceived
to be the preservation of the social *status quo,* but at the time of
Grotius the end of law was thought to be the enabling of individuals
to do things and possess things. The former conception stifled
individual creativity; the latter conception encouraged it.

Integral liberalism, as a political doctrine derived logically from
individualism, implied, therefore: (a) A belief that social control
is best secured by law rather than by command (this corresponds
to the dignity of the individual which entitles him to be ruled by

impersonal rules rather than by personal authority) ; (b) a belief in a natural order that embraces both the individual and the collectivity (the state) ; and (c) a belief that there is a sphere of rights, peculiar to individuals as human beings, beyond which the state cannot penetrate and for the preservation of which the state exists. These may be regarded as the criteria of integral liberalism.

Inherent in the notion of natural rights is the notion of natural liberty, the idea that the individual is free from limitation from all other individuals and from the state. This was a development from the Christian tradition, from the idea that there are certain spheres of individual life, particularly the religious and ethical, which are subject to limitation by God alone and never by the state. Now with the secularization of this idea, as it took place in the postulation of natural rights, particularly when the distinction between rights and interests was constantly blurred, anarchical tendencies emerged which, if not checked in some way, would lead to social chaos—to a war of all against all.

But to this subjective element in liberalism an objective one was counterposed. Not able to disregard the Christian tradition of which they were a part, Grotius and his successors believed that there were certain objective values, eternal truths, which were independent of individual will and interest. These they derived rationally from human nature or the "order of things." These objective values embodied in natural law constituted for Grotius and his contemporaries a limitation upon individual liberty.

Actually, then, two different legal theories are advanced : on the one hand, there is the notion that law is the product of individual wills and the embodiment of individual interests; on the other hand, there is the notion that law is the embodiment of eternal and absolute truths independent of either individual will or interest. In the first view men are conceived as submitting to law because they consent to, because their subjective interest compels them to do so ; in the other view, they submit to law because they recognize that it embodies certain absolute truths, that its content is just.

The two theories are logically independent of one another and self-sufficient. The force of historical circumstance merged them into one conception of law and for a time obscured their mutual inconsistency and independence. That Grotius and his contemporaries were not aware of this is not difficult to understand when one considers the intellectual milieu in which they lived and thought.[13]

The new age necessarily placed the individual at the center of its thought because it was particularly conscious of the reality of individuality. In every realm of activity men saw individuals creating things by their own energy. Behind law they saw individual will and interest. But at the same time they were not far enough removed from the medieval Christian tradition to believe that law was unrelated to absolute and eternal values. Their conscience, molded by Christian teachings, told them that law could not rest upon expediency alone, that obligation was rooted in the consciousness of certain eternal truths rather than in expediency or convenience.

They were unable, because of their Christian heritage and beliefs, to conceive of order as simply the product of the harmonizing of individual interests and wills. The medieval conception of a divine order unified by the will of God lingered in their consciousness and although they were aware of individuality, of individual will, in a way that no one was in the Middle Ages, they were incapable of conceiving of an order based upon this alone. Seventeenth-century mentality therefore merged the two concepts, despite their logical inconsistency and respective self-sufficiency, into one theory, which serves as a foundation for integral liberalism.

Now so long as men believed in objective truth and value transcending individuals, independent of individual wills and interests, so long as conscience was given a valid role in realizing the potential order embodied in reason, liberalism remained integral. It remained integral because there existed some objective and substantial limitation to individual will. Arbitrariness was excluded; responsible freedom was assured. When, however, men abandon the belief in transcendental standards, when the idea of objective truth and value is destroyed, liberalism becomes degenerate. The individualistic and subjective elements of liberalism are retained without the objective element that constitutes a limitation to arbitrariness. Freedom degenerates into license and irresponsibility, for freedom without responsibility is anarchy.

Law is obligatory, according to integral liberalism, because of its contents. Its contents are derived by objective reason which is capable of discovering eternal truth. It is conscience that bids the individual to reason objectively. Now when belief in objective value is abandoned, law can no longer be obligatory because of its contents. Concrete restriction of power is abandoned and only a formal restriction is retained. Men are no longer obliged to submit to law but compelled to do so. It is no longer conscience that dictates obedience but compulsion, the force behind the law rather than the content of the law. Physical compulsion is incompatible with human dignity and a purely formal restriction of power does not exclude arbitrariness nor guarantee the preservation of human rights. A liberalism that espouses—even by implication—these ideas may properly be distinguished from integral liberalism and designated as degenerate.

The logical structure of liberalism may be expressed diagrammatically as shown here.

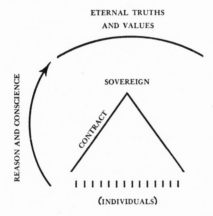

When, however, with the infiltration of positivism into all realms of thought, belief in the existence of eternal truths and values is lost and conscience is denied a valid role in the scheme of things the "liberal" is driven by his own logic to either of two conclusions: to make the sovereign absolute (tyranny) or to make the individual absolute (anarchy). The acceptance of a positivistic point of view drives the liberal to an espousal of irresponsibility either on the part of the state or on the part of the individual. For with the denial of values as positive facts, with all transcendental limitations to individual will denied, only a part remains (as shown in the accompanying diagram). The relationship between individuals

and the sovereign can no longer be regarded as a contractual one
for no means of interpreting the contract are left. Since justice
is a metaphysical concept the positivist "liberal" cannot evaluate

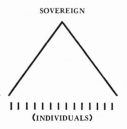

SOVEREIGN

(INDIVIDUALS)

the acts of the sovereign in terms of justice or injustice. Since he
denies the existence of eternal absolute human rights he cannot
evaluate the acts of the sovereign in terms of these. All basis of
obligation, as a matter of fact, disappears; compulsion is substituted for obligation. The positivist "liberal" has no choice but
to make the sovereign or the individual absolute. Ultimately his
own logic forces him, whether explicitly or not, to an espousal of
either tyranny or unbridled subjectivism.

THE SOCIOLOGICAL BASIS OF LIBERALISM

If liberalism is dependent upon modes of thought peculiar to the
age of individualism, it is equally dependent upon specific sociological conditions for its existence. For liberalism is not only a
mode of thought, it is a way of life. If its existence requires the
concept of the autonomous individual, it demands as well an environment congenial to the exercise of individual autonomy. As
social and economic conditions change so as to preclude the exercise of individual autonomy, liberalism as a way of life must
give place to a new way of life.

As a way of life, liberalism reflected the intellectual, social,
economic, and political aspirations and ideals of the rising commercial classes. In consequence the relationship between liberalism
and capitalism was an intimate one. But it would be a mistake to
see in liberalism only a convenient rationale for capitalism. For
the liberal ideology was something more than a mere excrescence
or mental reflex expression of an economic system. It was the embodiment of the seventeenth-century mentality and as much a

cause as an effect of the economic system that was developing at that time out of the collapse of feudalism. It was not simply an economic philosophy and way of life but a political, social, and intellectual philosophy and way of life as well. Liberalism and capitalism, moreover, developed concomitantly and simultaneously. And since capitalism is as much a system of ideas as it is a way of doing things it was as much the product of the mentality of the rising commercial classes as the mentality was the product of the system.[14] Both liberalism and capitalism are derived from the individualistic *Weltanschauung* that came into existence with the Renaissance and the Reformation.

Liberalism does have a specific sociological background but this includes a great deal more than economic factors. These constituted but one element of many influencing the mentality and institutions of the time. The arts, religion, science, and learning all contributed to the fostering of the mode of thought that gave rise to the liberal doctrine. Economic motives undoubtedly influenced the rising commercial classes but religious, social, and political motives were equally as important.

The early bourgeois was unsatiated, adventurous, confident, dissatisfied with the *status quo* and revolutionary. He was impressed not only with the potential creativeness of individual will but also with the dignity of human personality. His espousal of the rights of man was not simply the expression of a convenient conviction but of a belief in a way of life that he tended to regard as self-evident, but, if self-evident, yet not to be taken for granted but to be fought for.

If he rebelled with vehemence against the economic shackles imposed by mercantilism, he protested with equal fervor and conviction against arbitrary political power, Star chambers, *lettres de cachet,* inhuman treatment, and arbitrary restraints on his personal liberty. He was opposed to an aristocracy of birth not simply on economic grounds but as a matter of principle. He believed with conviction that certain actions and procedures violated the dignity which individuals possessed as human beings. This conviction was as much a part of his mentality as the desire for profits. If later on there was to be some conflict between the two attitudes, the rising commercial classes of the seventeenth and eighteenth century, at least, were not conscious of it.

The liberties which they demanded were not abstract liberties, for the rising commercial classes were rebelling not against injustice in the abstract but against specific actions, against concrete injustices. They did not protest against restraint of individual freedom in the abstract but against specific restraints. The concept of justice which they held was derived from innumerable specific instances of specific injustice. In Germany, for example, restraints like those imposed by the infamous Carlsbad decrees embodied all that the rising commercial classes regarded as unjust and against such restraints they rebelled with passionate conviction.

So long as the bourgeoisie remained economically, socially, and politically unsatiated they championed the substantial rights of man. As the social and economic system changed, as monopoly and finance capitalism replaced free enterprise and divorced control from ownership, and as the bourgeoisie acquired a dominant social and political position, they tended to espouse formal equality and formal rights of citizens rather than substantial equality and substantial rights of man. Legal rights tended to replace natural rights, equal application of the law tended to replace equal justice as a dominant concept, and freedom came to be regarded as freedom from illegal, but not necessarily, unjust compulsion.

THE FORMALIZATION OF LIBERAL THOUGHT

Detailed proof of the existence of integral liberalism in German political thought is given in the chapter which follows. It may simply be said here that since liberalism is the logical political expression of the individualistic *Weltanschauung* which has dominated all modern thought, it could not help but find manifestation in German political thought. And it did find in the thought of men like von Humboldt and Fichte, as well as in the thought of many of the men who attended the Constitutional Assembly of 1848, as fervent expression as it found in England and France.

To the integral liberal the universe was a rational one; it was pantheistic, and in place of the medieval dualism of a transcendent and a terrestrial world the new immanence philosophy posited the *coincidentia oppositorum*.[15] God remained as the Creator, but no longer as the Regent, of the universe. In the seventeenth and eighteenth centuries mathematical and physical theory was in the ascendancy and it was natural for men of that time, looking for

God, to find him immanent in nature rather than materially transcendent. As a keen literary critic has observed: "The poets, like
the astronomers and mathematicians, had come to regard the universe as a machine, obeying logical laws and susceptible of reasonable explanation: God figures merely as the clock-maker who must
have existed to make the clock."[16] God was the Great Mechanic of
a mechanism that ran by itself.

Integral liberalism maintained that the less one interferred with
this mechanical order the better. The government, therefore, that
imposed the fewest restraints upon individual activity was the
best. And the liberal economist declared: *laissez-faire et laissez-
passer, le monde va du lui-même.*

Towards the end of the eighteenth century, however, a reaction
set in, a Romantic reaction that felt this conception of a fixed
mechanical order to be a constraint upon individual activity.
Romanticism, conscious to the extreme of the particularity of each
occasion, revolted "against the whole of the mathematico-mechani-
cal spirit of science."[17] It was, with poetic mysticism, "directed to
the particular, the positive: to what is eternally productive of new
variety, constructive, spiritually organic; to plastic and super-
personal creative forces, which build from time to time, out of the
material of particular individuals, a spiritual Whole, and on the
basis of that Whole proceed from time to time to create the particular political and social institutions which embody and incar-
nate its significance."[18]

The effect of this Romantic movement was manifold; it extended
in every direction and into every realm of thought. It stressed the
importance of particular personalities rather than the common
humanity of individuals. It stressed emotion rather than reason.
It emphasized the collective mind, or *Volksgeist,* rather than individual reason. It focused attention on the nation, on national
culture, rather than on the universal community of mankind.

In the realm of political philosophy it led to a conception of the
state as "the embodiment and expression of a particular spiritual
world as it exists at a given time," and "the justice and law it
enforces" as "particular and positive."[19] Law becomes relative to
time and place, no longer universal, eternal, and absolute. "The
moral code," moreover, "is distinguished not only from the rules
of Law, but also from the demands and requirements of social

well-being."[20] This Romantic perspective finds expression in historical jurisprudence, in the writings of men like Savigny and Puchta.

Gradually, however, Romanticism gives way to positivism. In Germany the despotism that followed the War of Liberation and the added disillusionment that followed the collapse of the revolution of 1848 ushered in an age of realism, an age of Bismarckian *Realpolitik*. As Troeltsch observes:

From the idea of the particular law and right of a given time, men proceed to a merely positive acceptance of the State: morality of the spiritual order, transcending bourgeois convention, passes into moral scepticism; and the urgent movement of the German mind towards a political form and embodiment ends merely in the same cult of imperialism which is rampant everywhere. Caught in an obscure welter of motives, thought turned readily in the direction of Darwinism—a philosophy which, distorted from the ideas of its author, was playing havoc with political and moral ideas in western Europe as well as in Germany. Henceforth the political thought of Germany is marked by a curious dualism. . . . Look at one of its sides, and you will see an abundance of remnants of Romanticism and lofty idealism: look at the other, and you will see a realism which goes to the verge of cynicism and of utter indifference to all ideals and all morality; but what you will see above all is an inclination to make an astonishing combination of the two elements—in a word, to brutalize romance, and to romanticize cynicism.[21]

The subjective individualism of the Romantic movement greatly influenced the mechanistic ideas of the eighteenth century, although it never succeeded in replacing them, and when they were brought back into fashion again in the latter half of the nineteenth century it was with a different coloring.

In the latter half of the nineteenth century it was biology, rather than physics or mathematics, that contributed to a somewhat different conception of the natural order. The natural order was no longer conceived as a mechanism but as a biological organism. The result, however, was practically the same, for although this conception took cognizance of development and growth "it was the effect of the Theory of Evolution to reduce man from the heroic stature to which the Romantics had tried to exalt him, to the semblance of a helpless animal, again very small in the universe and at the mercy of the forces about him."[22]

Now the natural order, as conceived by integral liberalism, required individual reason for its realization since it was a potential order secured transcendentally in objective reason. But the natural order of the nineteenth century was something quite different; it was an immanent order which required no individual activity for its actualization. It was a product of materialistic forces which required neither reason nor an awareness of transcendental values for its existence.

This conception of the natural order was in large part the product of scientific materialism but it was also congenial to the nineteenth-century bourgeois way of life. Unlike their predecessors of the seventeenth and eighteenth centuries, the bourgeoisie were secure in political power, satiated, and content with the *status quo*. The conception of a static and immanent natural order provided them with the security and calculable certainty which they desired above all things. The bourgeoisie did not want change but preservation of the *status quo,* and if others clamored for change and reform, they could answer that change and reform by individuals could accomplish nothing. One must let things run their inevitable course.

This conception of the natural order was no less congenial to the way of life peculiar to nineteenth-century bourgeois society than the older conception was congenial to the revolutionary society of the rising commercial classes. Integral-liberal concepts were gradually formalized as the bourgeois attitude changed from an aggressive, unsatiated desire for individual autonomy to a satiated complacency and smug security which was put more and more on the defensive. Just as the concept of the natural order became formalized and abstract so the concepts of individual rights and of law became formalized and abstract.

However, it was not only as a result of a change in the position and way of life of the bourgeoisie that these concepts became formalized, but also as a result of the application of positivist, scientific modes of thought to social and political phenomena. The great technological advances which the physical sciences made possible in the nineteenth century not only increased the prestige and authority of the scientific method but stimulated men in other fields, students of law and of sociology particularly, to apply the same method to the study of social phenomena. They hoped to achieve for their fields of investigation the same prestige, the same calculability and certainty as characterized the physical sciences.

Natural law secured transcendentally and dependent upon rational recognition for its effectiveness was abandoned for a scientific "law of nature" secured immanently and effective independently of rational recognition. The existence of this "law of nature" could apparently be demonstrated empirically whereas "natural law" could not be, and this made it infinitely preferable to men of an age dominated by empiricism.

When applied to the study of law, the positive outlook of science, which in its extreme form denied the existence of values as scientifically relevant facts and which concentrated its attention on things which (it thought) could be observed without transcending experience, ended by positing positive law as the sole law and by denying the existence of an ideal law to which positive law should be made to conform. Positivism saw law as the product of will and distinguished law by the coercive force behind it. Coercion, rather than content, became the distinguishing characteristic of law.

The effect of positivism on liberalism was to encourage men to abandon a belief in objective values and thus to remove the limitation upon individual will which integral liberalism posited. Form rather than content occupied the attention of the positivist, and the legality of legal forms rather than the legitimacy of legal content was his chief concern. Technical efficiency and mechanical certainty replaced justice as the end of law. But with law divorced from some concept of substantial justice the way is prepared for social anarchy. Unless there is a conscious and voluntary affirmation of objective values for the attainment of which individuals will submit to a common authority, anarchy must inevitably follow.

Integral liberalism maintained that certain rights belonged to individuals by virtue of their humanity. Such rights were antecedent to the state. With the infiltration of positivism into politico-legal thought, in the latter half of the nineteenth century through the writings of jurists like Gerber, Laband, and Jellinek, individual rights were conceived as legal rights. They were no longer thought of as rights of human beings but as rights of particular citizens. The implication was that as concessions on the part of the state, which willed them into existence, they could be contracted away or even abrogated, if the state so willed. Individual rights, therefore, were thought of no longer as concrete, substantive limitations upon will but as purely formal limitations. Concessions, properly speaking, are not rights at all.

Positivism also tended to identify rights with interests. With the separation of law and ethics, legal rights tended to become identical with the stronger interest and will. Thus, by the turn of the century, liberty had become a formal concept, its content no longer determined by absolute values inherent in individuals as human beings but determined by the interests of the stronger.

To integral liberals "justice meant the securing of absolute, eternal, universal natural rights of individuals"[23] but to the nineteenth-century liberal it meant "the securing of the maximum of self-assertion."[24] The right of self-assertion was no longer deduced from the moral qualities or reasonableness of human beings, but was derived analytically from the abstract concept of liberty or was "found" in history.

As a result of emptying the concept of law of all substantive content, law became formalized; it became a mere formula suitable for any content. This, indeed, was the way in which the Neo-Kantians regarded it. Any government could be considered as *rechtsstaatlich* that marked off the power of the state from that of the individual through a formal commandment of law although the greatest inequality and injustice might actually result. A "liberalism" that espoused this view might properly be described as degenerate.

Emphasizing formal "equality before the law" and the general application of law as the criterion of a *Rechtsstaat*, late nineteenth century "liberals," as exemplified by Hans Kelsen, were completely unconcerned with the just or unjust content of law. Procedure and the manner of enactment replaced justice as the criterion of law. Integral liberalism held that the state exists to preserve human dignity and individual autonomy, to attain values that are inherent in individuals as human beings. With the sloughing off of objective values the atomistic and anarchial elements contained in liberalism came to the fore. The way was prepared for anarchy and for the dictatorship which is its political manifestation.

As Fritz Ermarth points out, one condition is indispensable to the functioning of liberal democratic parliamentary institutions, namely, "a fundamental, integrating idea" which serves to unite all citizens, "minority as well as majority."[25] With the formalization and subsequent degeneration of the liberal ideology that, despite its own inner weakness and attacks from rival ideologies, served this integrating function throughout the nineteenth century, the uniform basis upon which the will of the German people could be formulated was destroyed.

Intellectually and spiritually liberalism becomes degenerate by the acceptance of a positivistic point of view that destroys all objective limitation to subjective will. From such a point of view, individual rights no longer appear as objective, human attributes but as formal, legal concessions; the "natural" order that embraces both the individual and the state is no longer a potential, rational order requiring individual effort and recognition for its actualization but an immanent order requiring neither recognition nor individual effort for its operation; law appears simply and in the last analysis as the command of superior force. By denying the existence of values as facts, by regarding value judgments as expressions simply of subjective, individual preference or choice, positivism fosters intellectual anarchy and nihilism. It is just such a milieu that breeds fascism.

But if the fundamental postulate of liberalism—that of the absolute value of human personality—is undermined intellectually by positivism, it is destroyed socially and economically by those contemporary social conditions and institutions that emphasize the undesirability, if not the impossibility, of individual autonomy. In a simpler age individual autonomy was not only an ideal but a fact; in the complex, modern, industrial age individual autonomy is rapidly disappearing, both as a fact and as an ideal. And as conditions prove less and less amenable to individual efforts, the ideal of individual effort itself must necessarily appear impracticable. Without the ideal of the absolute value of human personality, without an environment congenial to the exercise of individual autonomy and responsibility, liberalism must, of necessity, disappear as a dominant and effective ideology.

The following chapters indicate, in some detail and with specific illustrations, how the liberal ideology became degenerate in Germany. They emphasize the forces and elements within liberalism itself that eventually brought about its own self-destruction.

CHAPTER II

INTEGRAL LIBERALISM

Es ist kein schön'rer Anblick in der Welt, Als einen
Fursten seh'n, der klug regieret; Das Reich zu seh'n,
wo jeder stolz gehorcht, Wo jeder sich nur selbst zu
dienen glaubt, Weil ihm das Rechte nur befohlen wird.
—GOETHE

LIBERALISM : THE POLITICAL EXPRESSION OF INDIVIDUALISM

LIBERALISM is premised upon the assertion of the absolute moral worth of each individual. It is the political expression of a comprehensive *Weltanschauung*, of an intellectual climate of opinion that has pervaded all realms of thought since the Renaissance. It is the theory of political order based upon individualism.

The individual seemed the proper starting point for many reasons. First of all, the early liberals lived in a cultural climate that was essentially Christian. The idea of the supreme worth of the individual, of all individuals everywhere, was contributed by Christianity through the notion of the salvation of individual souls. Each man was equal in the sight of God. When the Reformation destroyed the concept of an intervening hierarchy or priesthood between the individual and God and set man and God immediately in one another's presence, individual personality acquired even greater significance. For, when the Reformation posited the Church as "a fellowship of believers, each the direct concern of God, each directly responsible to God, each guided by the illumination of God in his own heart and conscience,"[1] responsibility for salvation devolved directly upon the individual.

This notion of the absolute value of human personality, of human dignity and worth, was coupled with the belief that all creativity springs from the individual. Ever since the Renaissance, when man rediscovered his ego, he has been conscious, as he never was in the Middle Ages, of his own will and of his power to create things for their own sake and for his own pleasure. As men turned from a theistic concept of God to a deistic concept (in which God was conceived as the Creator but no longer as the Regent of the universe), it was possible to ascribe greater freedom of will to

---

[1] For notes to chap. ii, see pp. 127–131.

individuals. And when deism gradually gave way to pantheism and God became absorbed in the material world still greater emphasis could be placed upon individual autonomy. As God was conceived less and less as a Creator, man was conceived as having more and more powers of creation.

Wherever men looked they saw individuals creating things. Individual initiative seemed particularly creative in the economic realm. Here a new order was rising upon the ruins of an old one by what appeared to be the sheer will and adventurous daring of individuals. With the introduction of private enterprise and the replacing of a rigid system based on status by a more flexible system based on contract, individual initiative was given wider scope. The fetters of privilege based on birth and social position were rent asunder by rebellious individuals.

The rising commercial class began now to talk about rights peculiar to individuals as human beings. They spoke of the right to possess things which they had acquired by their own labor, of the inviolability of the human body, of the freedom to speak and to write, of the right of peaceable assembly, and of the right of private property. But this was not only a convenient doctrine, it was one which actually reflected their way of life, their aspirations, and their mode of thinking. It was at once an intellectual doctrine derived logically from the premises of individualism and a reaction against specific abuses and injustices imposed by an absolute, mercantilist political and social order.

Just as the natural scientist regarded atoms, so the political philosopher regarded individuals as irreducible, self-sufficient entities deriving their nature from themselves and not from their relationships. In both cases it is "essences," and not "functions," that are regarded as determining the nature of reality. That men should look for "essences," for irreducible elements, when attempting to analyze social life is understandable when one considers that the age which followed the Renaissance was dominated by the concepts and methodology of modern science. Having returned to an atomistic conception of reality in the physical sciences it was natural for men to apply similar conceptions in other fields. As Lindsay says:

The great prestige of the new physical sciences produced continuous attempts to apply their method to the study of man in his social relations. Such a scientific study of society will tend to treat individuals as independent units. Each will be regarded as an atom, something having it own nature complete in itself. If they are to be scientific units they will have to be atoms identical in qualitative character. Because the theory will be interested mainly in the laws of the combination of such units it will tend to regard the units as equal?

But the doctrine of "human equality," he hastens to explain, "is in one sense not a scientific doctrine."[3] The doctrine rests essentially upon an ethical basis, upon the Christian concept of individual souls, and although the scientific method, as applied to the study of social relationships, gave assurance to an affirmation rooted in religious belief, it did not originate the concept. As the same author puts it: "The assumptions of scientific method . . . confirmed a doctrine whose real origin was in religious and not in scientific individualism."[4]

Individuals were conceived to be autonomous, each being a moral entity possessing an absolute value equal to that of every other individual, and it followed logically that arbitrary, capricious authority over individuals was incompatible with this concept. If each individual was to be able to realize his full moral value, to command the respect due him as a human being, he could not submit to any will that was arbitrary or capricious, for such submission would be a denial of moral autonomy.

Liberalism, as the political expression of individualism, therefore espoused freedom for the individual from all personal, arbitrary authority. Starting from the premise of the absolute value and dignity of human personality, liberals necessarily demanded freedom for each individual from every other individual, from the state, from every arbitrary will. Only when liberalism coupled the contract theory with the belief in objective truth and value, transcending all individuals and binding upon each without promise, could it reconcile freedom from arbitrary authority with the idea of an ordered commonwealth.

Liberalism in its integral form, therefore, starting from the premise of the absolute value of human personality, demands freedom for each individual from all personal, capricious, and arbitrary authority. Since freedom degenerates into license without some notion of responsibility and since submission to any individual will is incompatible with the postulate of human dignity and equality, it follows that freedom can only be secured through an impersonal authority, through a law that is found and not made. Integral liberalism, therefore, espouses freedom for each individual under the law, the law being conceived as embodying certain substantive and eternal truths transcending all individuals and binding upon each without promise.

THE PERVASIVENESS OF INDIVIDUALISM

To understand how completely modern thought has been submerged in the *Weltanschauung* of individualism, it will suffice if a few examples, from various realms of thought, are given. Since individualism has permeated all thought since the Renaissance, it is clear that every thinker of the modern age has made some concession to it. Individualism, as a climate of opinion, colored the thought of all Western civilization; it was not confined to one realm of thought alone or to any one particular nation. It found expression in Germany just as it found expression in England, France, America, and the other nations of the Western world. The antinomy between body and soul, man and nature, the one and the many, object and subject (product of the individualistic *Weltanschauung*), was an antinomy with which all thinkers of all the nations of the Western world were concerned.

Conservatives as well as liberals focused their attention on the individual, and even though the socialists seem, at first glance, to repudiate the prevailing *Weltanschauung,* in fact they do not. They accept, as do all thinkers of the age, the antinomy between man and nature, the one and the many, the individual and society; they emphasize the social rather than the individual element, but they accept the same dichotomy. They view the same problem from a different angle. Probably it is only the functionalists who have rejected this *Weltanschauung,* and they are of recent vintage.

All modern thinkers, with the exception of the functionalists, have agreed in placing the individual at the center of their thought. Most of them have posited a free-willed, autonomous, rational individual through whom alone creative forces could be put to work. Progress, until recently, has been considered as inevitable and as proceeding through the perfection of individuals. Progress, moreover, has been measured in terms of individual values, and although the socialists emphasize reform through the group, rather than by private initiative, the success of their endeavor is measured in terms of benefits to individuals. The betterment of individual conditions, spiritual and economic, is an essential aim of socialism. It does not abandon the individual but seeks rather to bring about conditions under which it believes the individual will be able to realize himself more fully, share more fully in material goods, and attain the economic security and well-being requisite to human dignity.

Individual values have found their place in conservative Hegelianism and in Marxian socialism, as well as in liberalism. Some writers have emphasized the collectivity, rather than the individual, but they have been able to do so only by accepting as fundamental the antinomy between the one and the many. They have focused their attention on one side of a "two-headed coin" but they have been able to do so only by positing a "two-headed coin" to start with. Some writers have emphasized nature, rather than man, but they have been able to do so only by first presupposing a fundamental antinomy between man and nature. Some writers have emphasized man as a physical entity, rejecting his spirituality, but again they have been able to do so only by accepting a fundamental antinomy between soul and body. With the exception of the functionalists, all modern thinkers have started from this dichotomy. The differences between schools of thought have been differences in emphasis, not in conceptual presuppositions. These conceptual presuppositions are those of individualism, and it is in this perspective that all modern thinkers have endeavored to explain and understand their physical, spiritual, and social environment.

The doctrine of individualism has a parallel in the atomistic perspective of physical science. Until recently physical scientists believed that "it is possible to describe all natural phenomena in terms of simple forces between unalterable objects."[5] Indeed, "throughout the two centuries following Galileo's time such an endeavor, conscious or unconscious, is apparent in nearly all scientific creation."[6]

As late as the middle of the nineteenth century Helmholtz declared:

Finally, therefore, we discovered the problem of physical material science to be to refer natural phenomena back to unchangeable attractive and repulsive forces whose intensity depends wholly upon distance. The solubility of this problem is the condition of the complete comprehensibility of nature.[7]

This mechanical view of natural phenomena, resting on the assumption of irreducible elements or atoms, found expression in the kinetic theory of matter, in the theory of electric fluids, and in the corpuscular and wave theories of light.[8] Atomistic ideas were introduced into chemistry by Lavoisier and John Dalton; the "cell" theory found expression in biology through the work of men like Johannes Mueller, Schleiden, and Schwann, and was carried into the idea of "organism" by Louis Pasteur.[9] Throughout the greater part of the nineteenth century these atomistic, mechanical theories remained practically unquestioned and dominant. All natural phenomena were thought of as being reducible to certain fundamental elements possessing certain attributes peculiar to them as particular and unique entities.

Similar notions pervaded other realms of thought. In response to the intellectual climate of opinion ushered in by the Renaissance and Reformation, theologians sought to overcome the rigidity of orthodox Christianity and to bring its principles into harmony with the dominant scientific thought and with the individualistic milieu. Liberal Protestantism "tended to brush aside all intermediaries—priests and prelates; sacred images and sacred relics; saints, angels, archangels, and even the Blessed Virgin herself— and so set God and the individual immediately in one another's presence."[10] Liberal theologians like Schleiermacher, for example, sought to make religion a matter of private feeling, an individual experience that did not rest upon intellectual demonstration or proof.[11]

Religion was made more and more a matter of private concern and the church gradually became a kind of fellowship where individuals met to do homage to God in their own way. It tended to become a meeting place for individual worship rather than a symbol of the collective affirmation of certain religious beliefs. The doctrine of "private judgment" in time became the doctrine that each individual could believe what he wanted to believe, worship as he wanted to worship, and give expression to his religious convictions any way he saw fit. Liberal theologians placed more and more emphasis upon religion as an individual experience, and less and less emphasis upon the church or the Bible as symbols or embodiments of divine truth. As one contemporary theologian has expressed it: "The Reformation had granted to the individual the 'right of private judgment' upon the meaning of the authoritative scriptures; the Enlightenment went further, and made the individual reason and conscience the final court of appeal, supreme over all external authorities."[12] With the destruction of the substantive content of conscience and the diminishing of faith in reason which took place in the latter part of the nineteenth and early part of the twentieth centuries, this "final court of appeal" tended to disappear.

In the realm of economic thought the individual was similarly the focal point. One of the first to espouse the optimistic doctrine that the general welfare is nothing but the resultant of private, individual interests was Adam Smith. The point from which he begins his whole theory is the individual. It is enlightened self-interest, he believes, which should be given the greatest possible freedom from arbitrary authority in order to express itself and to realize the potential harmony embodied in the nature of things. For, he wrote, man in pursuing self-interest "is in this as in many other cases led by an invisible hand to promote an end which has no part of his intentions."[13] He believed, as Gide and Rist say, that "natural economic institutions are not merely good; they are providential."[14] Without this belief in Providence, this belief in certain truths and values transcending individuals, Smith's "natural liberty" would be natural anarchy; his "freedom," license. To the anarchic element of his individualism he opposed this concept of a natural order filled with eternal, universal, and immutable truths. Individuals were to be free but free only to realize the potential harmony embodied in nature. It was not license which he espoused but responsible freedom, freedom under the law, a law which he conceived to be natural and to have substantive content.

It is significant, moreover, that Smith insisted on preserving the natural liberty of *individuals* and opposed strenuously every kind of collective enterprise, such as joint-stock companies, from which he believed individual self-interest was absent.[15] "The only exceptions which he would tolerate," write Gide and Rist, "are banks, insurance companies, and companies formed for the construction and maintenance of canals or for supplying great towns with water, for the management of such undertakings can easily be reduced to a kind of routine 'or to such a uniformity of method as admits of little or no variation.' "[16] It was not freedom for corporations, but freedom for individuals, which Smith espoused. The end of economic action is the individual and for this reason he should be let alone to follow the dictates of enlightened self-interest, to realize the potential harmony embodied in natural liberty.

This view is echoed again and again in economic thought, not only in England but in France and Germany as well.[17] Not only were there economists in Germany, like Schlettwein (1731–1802) and Schmalz (1760–1831),[18] who espoused economic individualism before or at the same time as did Smith in England, but also there was a large group of German economists who became champions of Smith's ideas after they became known in Germany.

One of the most ardent of this latter group was Christian Jakob Kraus (1755–1807), for a time a professor at the University of Koenigsberg in East Prussia. He declared on one occasion that Adam Smith's *Wealth of Nations* was the most important book after the Bible.[19] His enthusiasm was shared by others, particularly by those reformers who were gathered around Stein and Hardenberg, and one of them, the Freiherr von Vincke, wrote in his diary that he made it a daily habit to begin each day's work by reading a chapter in the "divine Smith."[20]

Kraus, like Smith, focused his attention on the individual and said that the national economy should be thought of as the sum of the private economic enterprises of the individual members of the state.[21] He regarded the national economy as functioning primarily for the benefit of the individual and, like Smith, conceived of the general welfare in terms of the welfare of individuals. Similiar views exhibiting a basic individualistic temper were expressed by German economists like Sartorius, Lueder, Jakob, Hufeland, Soden, Lotz, and Rau.[22] The theories of all of these writers, as Köhler remarks, strive to attain one goal, namely : *"die Wirtschaft durch den Geist der individualistischen Ethik zur Politik zu machen."*[23]

In the realm of political theory, too, the individual was placed at the center of thought. Professor Sabine sums it up well when he says :

The individual human being, with his interests, his enterprise, his desire for happiness and advancement, above all with his reason, which seemed the condition for a successful use of all of his other faculties, appeared to be the foundation upon which a stable society must be built. . . . Not man as a priest or a soldier, as the member of a guild or an estate, but man as a bare human being, a 'masterless man,' appeared to be the solid fact. . . . Society is made for man, not man for society; it is humanity, as Kent said, that must always be treated as an end and not a means. The individual is both logically and ethically prior. To the philosophy of the seventeenth century relations always appeared thinner than substances; man was the substance, society the relation. It was this assumed priority of the individual which became the most marked and the most persistent quality of the theory of natural law, and the clearest differentia of the modern from the mediaeval theory. Developed especially by Hobbes and Locke, it became a universal characteristic of social theory down to the French Revolution and maintained itself far beyond that date. It persisted, moreover, as a presumption in Bentham's School long after David Hume had destroyed the methodology of natural rights.[24]

Perhaps one of the most ardent individualists among German political thinkers was Wilhelm von Humboldt. He wrote:

Reason cannot desire for man any other condition than that in which each individual not only enjoys the most absolute freedom of developing himself by his own energies, in his perfect individuality, but in which external nature even is left unfashioned by any human agency, but only receives the impress given to it by each individual of himself and his own free will, according to the measure of his wants and instincts, and restricted only by the limits of his powers and his rights.[25]

His individualism was as extreme as that of Spencer and Mill (who was greatly influenced by von Humboldt) in England. But his belief in the moral uniqueness of individuals, his desire to treat each individual as an end in himself, was shared by many Germans and particularly by Kant and Fichte.

As a basic law of all human conduct Kant adopted the principle: "so act as to treat humanity, whether in thine own person or in that of any other, in every case as an end withal, never as a means only."[26] And Fichte declared: "Whatsoever does not violate the rights of another, each person has the right to do, and this, indeed, constitutes each person's *right*. Each one, moreover, has the right to judge for himself what is, and to defend, by his own powers, what he so judges to be, the limit of his free actions."[27]

We have seen that the concept of individuality permeated the whole fabric of thought which emerged with the Renaissance. It is found in science, in theology, in economic and political theory; it is found in England, in France, and in Germany.

INDIVIDUALISM AND NATURAL RIGHTS

From the presupposition that individuals are moral entities it followed logically that they must have some inviolable rights as human beings, that they are entitled as human beings to do certain things and to possess certain things if they are to realize their potentialities as individuals. Although there was some idea of rights peculiar to corporations and groups in the Middle Ages, the idea of natural rights peculiar to individuals first emerged as a definite concept in the seventeenth century. Since by that time the concept of God was gradually being replaced by the concept of nature, as deism replaced theism and in turn was giving way to pantheism, men called the immutable rights which they believed to be inherent in individuals by virtue of their humanity, *natural* rights.

By the thinkers of the seventeenth and eighteenth centuries "natural rights were felt to rest on the same basis as Newton's discoveries; and reason discerned these rights despite their daily violation, just as reason discerned the true movement of the earth despite its apparent immobility."[28] These rights were generally stated to consist of the right to life, liberty, and property. As gradually codified, they included such rights as freedom of worship, of speech, of press, and of assembly. By most of the writers of the age the existence of these rights was considered to be more or less self-evident, inherent in the nature of man and demonstrable by reason.

Belief in natural rights was essentially "an assertion that certain human desires have greater validity than, and must therefore prevail over force or circumstances or mere being."[29] And the fact that they were said to be grounded in human nature, that they were deduced in a sense from the nature of things, gave them "something of the prestige of physical, earthly existence" and the doctrine "could claim to be both a standard and a fact."[30]

Many writers, in endeavoring to prove the existence of natural rights, posited the existence of a "state of nature" antecedent to civil society in which individuals lived in a "natural" state and possessed rights which were peculiar to them as human beings. Locke, for example, posited a "state of nature" in which reason ruled supreme, and he believed that it taught those who would consult it "that being all equal and independent, no one ought to harm another in his life, health, liberty, or possessions."[31] It is important to realize that the early liberals did not conceive of the right to property as did the nineteenth-century liberals. Property was defined by Locke, for example, as that with which one had mixed his labor. It was not the right to receive dividends from stocks and bonds that the early liberal demanded, nor the right of impersonal business corporations to do with "their" property what they liked, but rather the right of a man to make himself economically secure by his own labor. The early liberal appreciated the fact that liberty without economic security was meaningless, and it was for that reason that he linked the right to property (to the fruits of one's own labor) with life and liberty.

To seek to explain seventeenth-century liberalism in terms of nineteenth-century conceptions of property and individual rights, as many writers do, is to mistake a distorted form of liberalism for integral liberalism. In an overzealous attempt to "explain" everything in terms of economic determinism, some writers, in effect, credit the seventeenth-century liberal with the ability to foresee social and economic developments of the nineteenth century, and, further, attribute to him the ulterior motive of providing a rationale for what was to take place two hundred years later! If liberal concepts were used in the nineteenth century to justify economic license, this is no indictment of integral liberalism, but more properly an indictment of those nineteenth-century "liberals" who perverted original liberal concepts to their own advantage.

Locke presupposed that men were equal in the sense that each individual was a moral entity, an end in himself, and he posited the existence of rights deduced rationally from this premise. "Every one," he wrote, "as he is bound to preserve himself, and not to quit his station willfully, so by the like reason, when his own preservation comes not in competition, ought he as much as he can to preserve the rest of mankind, and may not, unless it be to do justice on an offender, take away, or impair the life, or what tends to the preservation of the life, the liberty, the health, limb, or goods of another."[32]

These rights to life, liberty, and property Locke regarded as inalienable, as attributes of personality, as essential to human dignity. They were binding, he believed, on both society and government, and should the government attempt arbitrarily to dispose "of the lives, liberties, or fortunes of the people" he thought that the people were justified in dissolving the old government and acquiring a new one, by revolution if necessary.[33]

So strong was this belief in rights peculiar to individuals as human beings that it survived attacks made on the rationalistic basis upon which those rights had been originally posited. Even when the rights were no longer regarded as "natural," their existence was not questioned. Belief in a system of rights peculiar to individuals, although "explained" and justified differently, extended into the nineteenth century. Men like Bentham and Mill, for example, thought that individual rights were simply a matter of historical fact, that Englishmen had always possessed such rights. They justified them on the grounds of history, utility, heredity, and so forth.[34] However, they explained and justified these rights, few thinkers in the eighteenth and the early part of the nineteenth centuries doubted that individuals did possess inalienable rights peculiar to them as human beings. This was true not only in England but also in France, in Germany, and, indeed, throughout most of the Western world.

In France the doctrine of natural rights found eloquent and practical expression in the famous Declaration of the Rights of Man and Citizen of August 26, 1789. The preamble to that declaration declared:

The representatives of the French people, organized in National Assembly, considering that ignorance, forgetfulness, or contempt of the rights of man, are the sole causes of the public miseries and of the corruption of governments, have resolved to set forth in a solemn declaration the natural, inalienable, and sacred rights of man, in order that this declaration, being ever present to all the members of the social body, may unceasingly remind them of their rights and duties; in order that the acts of the legislative power and those of the executive power may be each moment compared with the aim of every political institution and thereby may be more respected; and in order that the demands of citizens, grounded henceforth upon simple and incontestable principles, may always take the direction of maintaining the constitution and welfare of all.

And even Rousseau, who wavered between authoritarian collectivism and extreme individualism, on one occasion declared:

To renounce one's liberty is to renounce one's quality as a man, the *rights* and also the duties of humanity. For him who renounces everything there is no possible compensation. Such a renunciation is incompatible with man's nature, for to take away all freedom from his will is to take away all morality from his actions.[35]

Earlier, in Germany, Christian Wolff was likewise espousing a belief in rights peculiar to individuals as human beings. "Nature," he wrote, "makes it incumbent upon men to perfect themselves."[36] Since the primary command of nature is "perfect thyself," one should perfect himself both morally and physically. Men have three duties, a duty to themselves, a duty to their fellowmen, and a duty to God, and since duties imply rights it follows that there are certain inalienable and inherent human rights.[37]

Similar views were held by von Humboldt. In order that the individual might be given the greatest possible freedom to perfect himself, von Humboldt urged that all restrictions on individual freedom be removed except those that were essential "to prevent encroachment upon his rights."[38] And Fichte asks: "What constitutes a free person, or what is requisite to make a person free?"[39] He answers that it is the possession of certain rights. These rights, he says, "are involved in the mere conception of the person, as such, and in so far are called *Original* [or inalienable] *Rights.*"[40]

INDIVIDUALISM AND FREEDOM

Starting, then, from the assumption that each individual is a moral entity possessing certain substantive rights by virtue of his humanity, it follows logically that each individual ought to be free to develop all his potentialities as a human being. And since arbitrariness is incompatible with human dignity any subjection to the will of another individual, to the will of any personal, capricious authority, is incompatible with the idea that each individual is an autonomous being, equal in moral value with every other individual.

Freedom, however, logically implies responsibility. In order for each individual to have freedom, all individuals must recognize some common authority, some common responsibility. This authority, moreover, must be impersonal, calculable, and objective. Only through the acceptance by the individual of a common, impersonal, rational, and objective authority can the individual be said to be free.

When men of the seventeenth and eighteenth centuries were

confronted with this problem of freedom, explicitly or implicitly they reasoned in this way. Writing and thinking in an age that focused its attention on the individual as a moral entity, in an intellectual climate of opinion that espoused the individualistic *Weltanschauung* in every field of thought, they were compelled logically to the conclusion that freedom from personal, arbitrary, authority was essential to the dignity of human personality.

But the problem of freedom was more than a theoretical one, more than a logical deduction from presuppositions which they consciously or subconsciously accepted as eternally true. Individuals of the seventeenth and eighteenth centuries were hedged in and restrained politically and economically by arbitrary and personal authorities. This restraint not only impeded the expansion and development of free private economic enterprise, but also it appeared incompatible with the dignity of human personality. The rising commercial class rebelled against these restraints. At first it supported the absolute monarchs, but as it became stronger and more self-assertive, it turned against them. Self-confident, eager for conquest, and adventurous, the commercial class found the restraints imposed by absolutism incompatible with its economic, social, and intellectual aspirations. Arbitrary control of economic activity, especially when exercised by an absolute monarch, was unpredictable and unstable. Commercial activity could flourish only under conditions that were predictable, calculable, and stable. There must be some order but this order needed to be impersonal, beyond the will of any arbitrary individual.

In order to realize their conception of individual autonomy and in order to carry on their struggle against absolutism, the rising commercial classes needed freedom to express their views, to assemble freely, to be free from arbitrary arrest and imprisonment, and to have a voice in the shaping of governmental policy. But their espousal of individual natural rights was more than a convenient doctrine; they espoused civil liberties and representative government because these things were essential if absolutism was to be defeated. In their own minds they probably did not separate the social and intellectual from the economic motives; all these prompted their ardent advocacy of civil and political liberties, for all were present and sprang ultimately from the concept of individuality which emerged with the Renaissance and Reformation.

Their attitude was at once the product of logical derivation from philosophic premises and of social and economic interests. It was at once a theoretical intellectual attitude and a practical expression of rebellion against concrete restraints and specific injustice.

Liberalism was the political expression of this attitude. In its name one can discern the core of its thought—freedom (*libertas*). Freedom from what? Freedom from arbitrary, personal authority; freedom from other individuals, from the state, from every authority that is personal or capricious. Intellectually it was the logical outgrowth of the individualistic *Weltanschauung;* politically and economically it was the embodiment of reaction against mercantilism and absolutism.

LAW AS THE BASIS OF FREEDOM

The central problem with which liberalism is concerned is the relation between the individual and authority. Liberalism holds that the individual should be free, but realizes that freedom demands the common acceptance of an impersonal authority if it is to be freedom and not license. Accordingly, liberalism espoused freedom from every form of social control except law. As Voltaire succinctly put it: "Freedom exists in being independent from everything but law."[41]

The authority, which necessarily had to be impersonal, objective, and independent of will, could be nothing else than law. Law, moreover, had to be conceived as eternal, immutable, and rational. If the authority was not to be arbitrary, it could not emanate from any will that was capable of acting capriciously; it could not change from day to day or place to place; it must be rational and predictable. It was found, but not made, by reason and by conscience.

Implicit in this reasoning is the assumption that positive law will conform to certain norms and values secured transcendentally, and the further assumption that the enforcement of law is purely impersonal and technical. In this assumption concerning the enforcement of law there is already an element of formalism, a quantitative conception of justice, but the notion of natural rights is a qualitative conception, and in the beginning this latter conception overshadowed the former.

Accordingly, two essential elements are found in liberalism in its integral form : first, the belief that society is composed of atomic, autonomous individuals; and, second, the belief that there are certain eternal truths transcending individuals and independent of either individual will or desire. These eternal truths are referred to by the writers of the seventeenth and eighteenth centuries as natural law or natural rights, but writers of the early nineteenth century arrived at a similiar conception in somewhat different terminology. Positive law, in either view, is legitimate and capable of commanding obligation if its content conforms to the content of these transcendental truths.

Positive law is not binding simply because it emanates from the legitimate sovereign, for the sovereign, like all individuals, is under a higher law. He cannot act arbitrarily and cannot make his will binding on other individuals unless his acts fall within the limits set by the higher law. The individual can know if the sovereign is acting justly—if his acts fall within the limits set by law—only through conscience, for it is by objective reason that the individual recognizes the content of law and conscience alone bids him reason objectively. Obligation, accordingly, rests essentially upon individual conscience. The contract does not bind the individual to obey blindly all the commands of the political sovereign, for if the sovereign acts unjustly, if he oversteps the limit set by law, the contract is void and his subjects may legitimately depose him.

It is the duty of individuals to reason objectively, to subordinate passion and desire, in order to recognize the limitations upon will which alone make freedom possible. The content of law is discovered by dispassionate reason, but only conscience obligates the individual so to reason. The link, therefore, between transcendental norms, which constitute the only limitation upon will, and individual will is conscience.[42]

One of the earliest modern writers to describe this concept of law was Grotius. In the early part of the seventeenth century he wrote :

Natural law is the dictate of right reason. . . . It is to be remarked that the law of nature deals not only with things which are outside of the human will, but also with things produced by the act of man. Thus property, as it now exists, is the result of human will; but being once introduced, the law of nature itself shows that it is wrong for me to take what is yours against your will. . . . The law of nature is so immutable that it cannot be changed even by

God himself. . . . God himself cannot make twice two not be four; and in like manner He cannot make that which, according to reason, is intrinsically bad, not be bad.[43]

Although he believed that the eternal truths embodied in the natural law were immutable, by man or God, at the same time he believed that they had their source in human nature, that is, that they depended for materialization upon the exercise of creative individual reason and conscience. "The mother of natural law," he wrote, "is human nature itself."[44] Right is what is in accordance with reason, and since man is endowed with reason by virtue of his being human, even if there were no God, the realization of right would rest entirely upon individuals.[45] The link between subjective will and objective truth and value is human reason and conscience. The responsibility for realizing the potential order embodied in nature rests upon the willingness of individuals to reason rightly, to follow the dictates of reason and conscience. This is the cardinal element of the liberal conception of law.

For the liberals, human conscience is the source of law and order. They start "from the conviction that man [is] not only a physical being, subject to natural laws, but also a moral being subject to his conscience . . . freedom [is] not arbitrariness but subjection to the moral nature of man, which is governed by the moral law. Freedom is accordingly only to be found in subjection to reason, that is to say, man is free only when all his actions are determined by reason."[46]

The immediate followers of Grotius in the seventeenth and eighteenth centuries differed somewhat from him in describing the content of natural law, but few, if any, doubted its existence and most agreed on defining it as the dictate of right reason. Just as the natural scientist of the age believed that there were universal, eternal principles governing the physical universe, so the political philosophers of the same period believed that there were similar principles governing human existence. In both science and philosophy, these principles were considered to be independent of human will, although discoverable by human reason. It was thus possible to equate jurisprudence with ethics, "to think of legal precepts as a specialized type of moral precept."[47] In the seventeenth and eighteenth centuries, as Roscoe Pound says, "jurists believed that a complete and perfect system of legal precepts could be built upon principles of natural law discoverable by reason and derived from the ideal of the abstract man."[48]

This law of nature was thought to be binding upon *all* individuals, and although the concept of sovereignty which emerged in the sixteenth century might seem at first, by its definition, to contradict this principle, actually it did not. Bodin defined sovereignty as the "highest power over citizens and subject, unrestrained by laws."[49] But, in spite of the phrase *legibus soluta,* Bodin recognized, as Max Shepard has pointed out, certain very definite limitations upon the sovereign.[50] These limitations can be divided into three main categories: (1) *leges naturae et divinae;* (2) *jus gentium;* and (3) *leges imperii.* As Bodin wrote:

... if we define authority as absolved from all laws, no prince is found to have the rights of sovereignty anywhere, since the divine law, and law likewise of nature, as well as the law common to all nations which has its reason derived from the law of nature and divine laws, holds all.[51]

In another place he observed:

As for the laws of God and of nature, princes and people are equally bound by them. . . . What we have said as to the freedom of sovereignty from the binding force of law does not have reference to divine or natural law.[52]

There was no idea that the monarch was not bound by natural law; on the contrary, he was as much bound by it as any other individual. The test of freedom was whether or not the legislator was subject to limitation, whether or not there was some limitation upon arbitrary will. If there were no such limitation, there could be no freedom. Freedom meant concrete and substantive limitations upon will, whether the individual will of a monarch or the collective will of a legislature. It did not mean a formal limitation but a *substantive* limitation.

When legislative assemblies emerged and began to transfer to themselves the concept of sovereignty which had first been espoused for absolute monarchs, they too were thought of as subject to certain definite limitations imposed by a higher law. Locke made this particularly clear. He held that the legislature was the supreme branch of government, but he said:

Though the legislative, whether placed in one or more, whether it be always in being or only by intervals, though it be the supreme power in every commonwealth, yet, first, it is not, nor can possibly be, absolutely arbitrary over the lives and fortunes of the people. *A man, as has been proved, cannot subject himself to the arbitrary power of another. . . . The law of nature stands as an eternal rule to all men, legislators as well as others.* The rules that they make for other men's actions must, as well as their own and other men's actions, be conformable to the law of nature.[53]

Tyranny, for Locke as for other liberals, was not synonymous with autocracy but rather with despotism. A government might be highly centralized and autocratic but so long as it recognized substantive limitation to its will it was legitimate. "Wherever law ends, tyranny begins," Locke declared.[54] It was not the form of government which determined its legitimacy, though one form might be preferred to another, but whether there was personal, arbitrary rule or the impersonal rule of law.

The idea of the liberal political philosophers that "the law" was a natural order filled with substantive content was shared by the economists of the seventeenth and eighteenth centuries, finding early expression particularly among the Physiocrats. According to one of them: "The natural order is merely the physical constitution which God Himself has given the universe."[55] "Its laws," according to another, "are irrevocable, pertaining as they do to the essence of matter and the soul of humanity. They are just the expression of the will of God."[56] Commenting on this conception Gide and Rist write:

It was just because the 'natural order' was 'supernatural,' and so raised above the contingencies of everyday life, that it seemed to them to be endowed with all the grandeur of the geometrical order, with its double attributes of universality and immutability. It remained the same for all times and all men. Its fiat was 'unique, eternal, invariable, and universal.' Divine in its origin, it was universal in its scope, and its praises were sung in litanies that might rival the *Ave Maria.*[57]

The idea of a natural order is carried over from the Physiocrats into classical economics by Adam Smith and perpetuated by his followers.

The theologians were similarly abandoning a theistic concept of authority and accepting more and more an immanent authority in the form of certain principles. As one writer has expressed it, although they gave up "the belief in God's extraordinary and miraculous intervention in human affairs" they "laid all the more stress upon God's regular and orderly government."[58] For the pessimistic outlook of orthodox Christianity they substituted an optimistic outlook. Whereas the orthodox Christian looked upon sin as the root of all evil, the liberal theologians tended to regard ignorance as the root of evil. Sin could be removed only by God and by grace; ignorance could be overcome by man through education. Orthodox theologians did not believe the world could be freed from evil, liberal theologians did. This optimistic belief in inevitable progress by education was shared by classical economists and liberal political philosophers.

Thus, in the fields of political philosophy, economics, and theology, emphasis was placed in the seventeenth and eighteenth centuries upon an impersonal natural order which could be realized by human reason and conscience. On the one hand, there was the autonomous individual, on the other, the potential order objectified in eternal and universal principles with conscience and reason as the link between the two.

LIBERALISM AND THE RECHTSSTAAT

These two elements found in integral liberalism, namely, the belief in politically autonomous, rational individuals, and the belief in eternal, universal truths secured in a natural order gave rise in Germany to a political concept which merged the two, the concept of the *Rechtsstaat*. Under the *Rechtsstaat* men were conceived to be free from all authority except that of law. Men were to be equally free from injustice and arbitrariness and equal before the law. Justice and legality were considered to be identical and to be independent of consent or personal will because the authority of law was essentially and completely impersonal and objective. Administration of the law was regarded as more or less mechanical.

The ideal of the *Rechtsstaat* is to provide each individual with the maximum possible freedom. Only law is to restrain him. An analogous idea is found in classical economics. Here each individual is to be given the greatest possible freedom from the state and from other individuals, and natural economic laws provide whatever regulation or restraint there is. As Adam Smith stated it: "Every man, *as long as he does not violate the laws of justice*, is left perfectly free to pursue his own interest his own way."[59] The idea espoused is one of freedom, but not of license. It is the idea that all artificial, personal restraint should be removed that man might act *in accordance with nature and its laws.* It is a belief in a pre-stabilized social harmony embodied in the natural order.

State regulation is considered bad because it interferes with this natural order. It is artificial and should function best as a negative agency, restraining and redressing injustice but taking no action to provide for the positive welfare of its citizens. Because there is a natural order embodying eternal, universal, and objective principles the government that governs least governs best. *"Laissez-faire et laissez-passer, le monde va du lui-même."*

The way in which liberals regarded the function of the state is perhaps best illustrated by Wilhelm von Humboldt in his *Ideen zu einem Versuch die Grenzen der Wirksamkeit des Staates zu bestimmen.*[60] The title of the book itself states the central problem with which they were concerned, namely, how to determine the limits of the activity of the state. So significant and dominant was this problem in the eighteenth century that Humboldt declared that "the inquiry into the proper aims and limits of state activity ... comprises the ultimate object of all political science."[61] At this time it was a foregone conclusion among liberals that the activities of the state should be limited, there only remained the question of how these activities should and could be limited. That government which governed least governed best was the premise from which all liberals started, for, as Humboldt declared, "those processes of human activity advance most happily to their consummation, which most faithfully resemble the operations of the natural order."[62]

The liberals denied that the state should exhibit any solicitude for the positive welfare of the citizen. "A state," wrote Humboldt, "has one of two ends in view; it designs either to promote happiness, or simply to prevent evil; and in this latter case, the evil which arises from natural causes, or that which springs from man's disregard for his neighbor's rights."[63] He denied that the state should endeavor to promote happiness in a positive way and argued that its function was simply to prevent evil, particularly the evil "which springs from man's disregard for his neighbor's rights." Humboldt listed three reasons why he believed state solicitude for the positive welfare of citizens to be harmful. First, he said, it "invariably superinduces national uniformity, and a constrained and unnatural manner of action."[64] Variety is sacrificed and, although it may lead to "comfort, ease, and tranquility,"[65] these things are not what men strive for. The individual does not want "inertness and uniformity"[66] but rather "the most perfect freedom of developing himself by his own energies, in his perfect individuality."[67] The second reason why he believed state paternalism to be harmful was that "state measures always imply more or less positive control; and even where they are not chargeable with actual coercion, they accustom men to look for instruction, guidance, and assistance from without, rather than to rely upon their own expedients."[68] Positive state action tended, he believed, to destroy individual initiative and self-reliance, and impeded individual self-realization and development. The third reason he gave was that "in proportion as each individual relies upon the helpful vigilance of the state, he learns to abandon to its responsibility the fate and well-being of his fellow citizens."[69] Individuals will not be as mindful of the welfare of others, he declared, if the state takes over a responsibility that is essentially an individual responsibility; kindliness and philanthropy will be destroyed. States which try to provide for the positive welfare of citizens, he says, "too often resemble the physician, who only retards the death of his patient in nourishing his disease. Before there were physicians, only health and death were known."[70] He implied that it was impossible for the state to cure an evil, the best it could do was ameliorate it. The root of evil was found in individuals and they and they alone could overcome it. It was best to let the "diseases" of society run their inevitable, natural course. He concludes therefore that "the state is to abstain from all solicitude for the positive welfare of the citizens, and not to proceed a step further than is necessary for their mutual security and protection against foreign enemies; for with no other object should it impose restrictions on freedom."[71]

Individuals need freedom in order to preserve their dignity as men but they also need security, Humboldt declared. By security he meant protection from "attacks of foreign enemies" and "the danger of internal discord."[72] These are things "which man is wholly unable to realize by his own individual efforts."[73] The state must perform these negative functions, for without security there can be no freedom, but the state has no other purpose, he declared. It "is not itself an end, but is only a means towards human development."[74] By providing security the state allows individuals to perfect themselves in freedom, and it may never "make man an instrument to subserve its arbitrary designs," nor "induce him to neglect for these his proper individual ends."[75] The state has no other purpose than to provide a milieu for individual advancement, it is a means for the attainment of ends which are essentially individual.

"It is evident," Humboldt wrote, "that political activity can only extend its influence to such actions as imply a direct trespass on the rights of others; to the task of deciding in cases of disputed right; to redressing the wronged, and punishing the wrongdoers."[76] The state exists to protect and guarantee individual rights, to uphold the dignity of personality, and to provide the conditions of the greatest possible individual freedom. The state should exhibit positive solicitude for the welfare only of those persons who are not in possession of their "natural faculties" such as immature persons and those who are mentally deranged or deficient.[77]

Humboldt declares that security might be defined as "the assurance of legal freedom,"[78] or, in other words, freedom under the law. Men should know what they can and cannot do, and the state should protect the rights of the individual, and redress the violation of those rights. Presupposed in this idea is the notion of impersonal law.[79]

It was out of this concept of law, as I have said, that the idea of the *Rechtsstaat* evolved. The *Rechtsstaat* embodies the idea of constitutional government, which McIlwain characterizes as "limited government."[80] Constitutional government does not, McIlwain insists, necessarily mean weak government nor is it inconsistent with autocratic government, for any government that recognizes substantive limitations upon its authority may properly be regarded as constitutional. As McIlwain says, the law which defines the limitations may be customary, unwritten, or embodied in a written document, but in any case there must be "a law that puts bounds to arbitrary will."[81] That is a characteristic of constitutional government and of the *Rechtsstaat* as well. The opposite of constitutional government is not autocracy, which might be regarded as "unmixed government," but rather despotism, that is, "lawless government."[82] Although in practice autocracy and despotism may tend to merge, they are not identical.

The autocratic monarchs, although not controlled, were nevertheless limited. This idea that there can be limitation where there is no political control was expressed in the thirteenth century by Bracton when he said:

> The King himself ought not to be subject to man, but subject to God and to the law, for the law makes the King. Let the King then attribute to the law what the law attributes to him, namely, dominion and power, for there is no King where the will and not the law has dominion.[83]

"As moderns," McIlwain writes, " . . . we tend to fix our attention on the legitimacy of an act of government, where the ancients looked merely to its desirability or expediency,"[84] And, he adds, that "such an idea of legitimacy could only arise after men had come to think of a universal law which had more coercive power than mere universal reason, but, like reason, was coterminous with mankind; and, what is more, coeval with man himself. And granted that there was such a preëxistent law, it became inevitable that governments and their acts should be judged by their conformity to it rather than to reason alone."[85] The idea of the *Rechtsstaat* and of constitutional government was a logical derivative from the idea of natural law. The function of the *Rechtsstaat* is to administer justice to all, *not merely to protect individual status but to establish every individual in his right status.* It is government by law, but government by *right* law.

This concept of the *Rechtsstaat,* particularly as formulated by Fichte, is the expression of integral liberalism, which espouses freedom for each individual under the impersonal authority of a law that transcends individual will or desire. It conceives of this law as having substantive content which serves as a limitation upon arbitrary will and as being discoverable through reason and conscience. To trace the development in Germany of liberalism one must trace the development of the *Rechtsstaatsidee* which is its embodiment.

Fichte continually stresses the fact that individual freedom can be obtained only by the common acceptance of a universal law. "All positive laws," he wrote, "are, in a greater or less degree, deduced from the rule of Rights *(Rechte).* There is and can be no arbitrariness in them. They must be such as every rational being would necessarily make them. In these positive laws the rule of

Rights is applied to the specific objects which the rule comprises. Positive law floats in the middle between *Rechtsgesetze* and *Rechtsurtheile*. In positive law the rule of Rights is applied to particular objects; in the decisions of law, the positive law is applied to particular persons."[86] That Fichte thought the administration of law was more or less mechanical is further indicated by his statement: "The civil judge has to decide only what has occurred, and then to state the law which applies to the occurrence. If the law is clear and complete, the decision or sentence should already be contained in it."[87]

Submission to law, he says, is not subjection "to the arbitrary will of a man, but to an unchangeable, determined will, in fact, to the will of reason in general, or to my own will, as that will must be, if determined by the rule of Rights; and unless my will is so determined, I have no rights at all."[88] But the difficulty, he says, is not yet completely solved. There must be some assurance that law *will* be supreme and that no power "except that of law can ever be turned against me."[89] He is in search, he says, "of a will which shall have power only where the law wills, and which shall have no power whatever where the law does not will; *a will*, in short, *which is an infallible power, but only when in conformity with the will of the law.*"[90]

The will which he finally posits as capable of performing this function is the united will of free persons associated in a commonwealth existing to guarantee the rights and freedom of each individual within it.[91] As he explains it:

That a number of free beings unite themselves, signifies: they desire to live together. But this they cannot do, unless each restricts his freedom by the freedom of all others. If a million men live together, it is very possible for each of them to desire as much freedom as possible. But if you unite the will of all of them in one conception, as one will, then that one will divides the amount of possible freedom in equal parts emong them all; desires all to be free, and hence desires the freedom of each to be restricted by the freedom of all others. The only possible point of union for their will is, therefore, the Law, and, in our case—where a fixed number of men of various inclinations and occŭpations live together—the Law, in its application to them, or their Positive Law. As sure as they are united they must will the law. If but one of them is wrongly treated, this one certainly protests, and they are no longer united. . . . Concerning justice and law, therefore, all are agreed; and all who are agreed necessarily desire law and justice. There cannot be a community, whereof one member has another will than the other member. But as soon as two individuals are no longer united in their will, at least one of the two is at variance with all the others; his will is an individual, and hence an unjust will. If the will of the other, with whom he is in conflict, agrees with the will of all the others, then this other is necessarily right.[92]

The substance of his concept is contained in the statement that "the existence of the commonwealth itself [should] be made to depend upon the effectiveness of the law."[93] In other words, individuals unite for the purpose of securing justice to each and the commonwealth can only exist so long as injustice is not tolerated. "The relation between each member and the commonwealth," he wrote, "must, therefore, be thus, that, from each injustice against an individual however petty, there also results, necessarily, injustice to all."[94]

Fichte apparently believed that this ideal *Rechtsstaat* could be established by the adoption of a written constitution. He did not believe that the form of government was necessarily prescribed although he did believe that democratic government was the least desirable form, because under it the people would be both judge and party.[95] He would have the people elect a tribunal, which he called an Ephorate, to watch over the government and decide when its acts were unconstitutional. He thought that this system was preferable to a separation of powers. Ordinary judicial power he would leave under the supervision of the executive; the Ephorate would function as a kind of super-tribunal sitting in judgment upon acts of the government. If the government acted unconstitutionally, the Ephorate would first issue a warning, and then, if the government did not heed the warning, it would call the people together in convention to overthrow the government.[96]

Too often has Fichte been unjustly described as an ideological forerunner of the National Socialists. Although his patriotism often led him to make assertions which, if extracted from the context of his political philosophy, sound similar to the boastings of the Nazis, Fichte's temperament and philosophy, his motives and his character, are diametrically opposed to everything the Nazis stand for. In a recent article which ably points this out, F. W. Kaufmann observes that "Fichte is a moral idealist whose principal concerns are the political and inner freedom of the individual, the right and duty of the individual to contribute his best to the welfare and the cultural progress of his nation, the independence of all nationalities, social security, and an acceptable standard of living for every human being. These demands are based on a genuine respect for the dignity of man and the desire to contribute to the rule of humanitarian values in all human relations."[97]

Of his *Reden an die deutsche Nation,* in which many writers have found evidence of Fichte's kinship with the Nazis, Kaufmann says :

> One may explain such extreme statements as products of a war psychology created by the presence of any army of occupation. What counts more, how-ever, is the fact that Fichte does not give a picture of what the German people really are, but what they should become in the future. It is his desire that they use the present crisis and their misery to reform their own individual and political life, to free themselves from external bondage, and to *become* the elect people in their striving for the realization of a spiritual community of man . . . the most fervently nationalistic of Fichte's works is not a prophecy of German racial preëminence, but a challenge to take the lead in responsible world-citizenship. Its spirit is diametrically opposed to that of National Social-ism. . . . Instead of finding in Fichte another proof for an incorrigible warlike German mentality, one should rather emphasize the undeniable fact that Na-tional Socialism betrays the best German tradition and debases the German character.[98]

Nationalism, as it was originally conceived by men like Fichte, Herder, and Mazzini, rather than being opposed to liberalism was its direct counterpart. The so-called "nationalism" of Hitler and of Mussolini is but a rank perversion of everything these men cherished and advocated.

A champion not only of national autonomy but of individual liberty and equality Mazzini told his fellow-countrymen :

> Your first duties—first as regards importance—are . . . towards humanity. You are *men* before you are either citizens or fathers. If you do not embrace the whole human family in your affection, if you do not bear witness to your belief in the unity of that family—consequent upon the unity of God;—and in that fraternity among the peoples which is destined to reduce that unity to action; if, wheresoever a fellow creature suffers, or the dignity of human nature is violated by falsehood or tyranny—you are not ready, if able, to aid the unhappy, and do not feel called upon to combat, if able, for the redemption of the betrayed or oppressed—you violate your law of life, you comprehend not that religion which will be the guide and blessing of the future.[99]

Mazzini was both a liberal and a nationalist. A nation, he said,

> . . . is not a mere zone of territory. The true country is the idea to which it gives birth; it is the thought of love, the sense of communion which unites in one all the sons of that territory.

So long as a single one amongst your brothers has no vote to represent him in the development of the national life, so long as there is one left to vegetate in ignorance where others are educated, so long as a single man, able and willing to work, languishes in poverty through want of work to do, you have no country in the sense in which country ought to exist—the country of all and for all. . . .

Never deny your sister nations. Be it yours to evolve the life of your country in loveliness and strength; free from all servile fears or sceptical doubts; maintaining as its basis the people; as its guide the consequences of the principles of its religious faith, logically and energetically applied; its strength, the united strength of all; its aim the fulfillment of the mission given to it by God.

And so long as you are ready to die for humanity, the life of your country will be immortal.[100]

LIBERALISM AND ADMINISTRATIVE CONTROL

Those German writers who followed Fichte suggested many different ways for bringing about a *Rechtsstaat,* but they were fundamentally in agreement with his idea of a commonwealth united under law for the purpose of securing justice to each individual. Such a state was necessarily a constitutional state, in the sense that it implied limitations on the powers of government, but it was something else as well. Men who came after Fichte were not certain that such a state could be established merely by the adoption of a written constitution. They were particularly plagued by the problem of how to make sure that the law would be binding on the executive, and they seemed more concerned about providing checks on the administration than providing checks on the legislature. This attitude was probably due to the conditions which prevailed in Germany, for the real threat to individual freedom came from the executive who was dominant and not from the legislature.

Otto Bähr, for example, wrote in 1864, that "to make the *Rechtsstaat* come true, it is not sufficient that public law be expressed in statutes; there must also be a judiciary qualified to establish what is right in the concrete case and thus give an indisputable foundation for the rehabilitation of law where it has been violated."[101] He suggested the establishment of a system of courts to administer public law, with the courts part of the ordinary judicial organization and judges both elected and appointed. His influence was not particularly great, however, and it remained for Rudolph von Gneist to give impetus to the movement for practical reform.

The chief conflict between private and public rights, Gneist insisted, did not come between the legislature and the individual but between the administration and the individual. Thus, he thought, the degree of freedom which the individual has is proportionate to the degree of control exercised over the administration. It was legal liberty, rather than political liberty, which particularly engaged his attention. He was particularly concerned with protecting individual rights, with providing machinery for the protection of these rights against executive and administrative power from which source he saw them most likely to be threatened.

Control over administration, he suggested, should first of all be legal, that is, administrators should know by statute what they can and cannot do. Secondly, administrators should administer law as though they were acting in a judicial capacity, not as partisans nor as agents of the ministry. Law interpretation and administration should be independent of the political administration and follow prescribed forms of procedure.

For Gneist the *Rechtsstaat* could only be achieved when "the whole inner administration of the State," was made independent "from the change of ministers, from the shifting of ministerial systems, from the irresistible tendency of the dominant party to make the possession of offices useful for vote-getting and party ends."[102] Having studied the English system, he was impressed with the political independence of the civil service, as well as with the system of local self-government, and urged the adoption of a similar system in Germany.

He admired as well the system of administrative law which he thought he saw developing in England. The adoption of a prescribed procedure, he thought, tended to make administration more responsible and provided individuals with recourse against the misuse of power. He advocated the establishment in Germany of administrative courts as part of the administrative organization although separate in the higher spheres from the ministry.[103] Three years after his book on the *Rechtsstaat* appeared, a Prussian Supreme Administrative Court with power to review executive measures was established in 1875. By aiding the development of administrative law it performed a function which constitutional law has performed in the United States.

For Gneist, as for Bähr, Lorenz von Stein, Robert von Mohl, and other German liberals, the state existed as but one association within society.[104] It was supreme over other associations only in the sense that it was conceived as existing to preserve unity among all the elements. It existed to provide individuals with the maximum possible freedom for self-development and self-expression. Ideally conceived, it was neutral in interest, serving only to administer justice. It existed not for the individuals within it conceived as a whole, but for *each* individual. It was the law of the state, administered alike to every individual, its content subject to substantive limitations, which guaranteed freedom for individuals with an ordered commonwealth based upon justice.

To summarize briefly: Liberalism in its integral form focused its attention on the individual as a moral entity, positing a belief in the absolute value of human personality. As a consequence, it demanded the greatest possible freedom for every individual from all authority that was personal, arbitrary, or capricious. It espoused freedom for the individual under the impersonal authority of law. It conceived of the law as being eternal, universal, and rational, and as containing substantive limitations upon subjective interest and will. To an anarchic conception of society as composed of autonomous individual units, liberalism opposed the conception of an order transcending individuals, and placed the responsibility for realizing this order, potentially embodied in eternal truths, upon individual reason and conscience. The link between the subjective will of the individual and the objective order transcending individuals was reason and conscience.

These original notions of liberalism found expression in Germany, as they did in every other nation of the Western world. With the formulation of the concept of the *Rechtsstaat*, and with the attempts made by men like Gneist to translate the idea into political reality, liberalism found practical as well as intellectual expression in Germany. In examining the development of the *Rechtsstaatsidee* in Germany, one necessarily examines the development of liberalism as a political doctrine.

CHAPTER III

THE INFLUENCE OF HISTORICISM AND POSITIVISM UPON ORIGINAL LIBERAL CONCEPTS

Das sogennante "positive" Recht ist . . . schlechthin Gewalt, physische Macht, der sich die Unterworfenen tatsächlich beugen . . . Denn aus den blossen Tatsachen des Befehlens, Gehorchens und Zwingens kann ebensowenig wie aus irgendwelchen Tatsachen und Kausalzusammenhängen ein Sollen gefolgert werden.

—RUDOLF LAUN

THE NINETEENTH CENTURY CLIMATE OF OPINION

IN THE COURSE of the nineteenth century, interest in the eternal gradually gave way to interest in the temporal, interest in the universal to interest in the particular and the relative. Attention shifted from man to his environment, from the "ideal" to the "real," from man in the abstract to man "as he actually is." Men saw chance and emotion operative in the world, as well as regularity and reason; they saw change and development, and within this development they "discovered" immanent principles of growth. This change in perspective was the result of two very different things. It was, in part, an outgrowth of a Romanticism that focused attention on the particularity of occasions, and, in part, an outgrowth of an endeavor to apply scientific methodology to a study of social phenomena. Both, for somewhat different reasons, stimulated the study of history and the search for particular and "positive" facts.

Romanticism discarded the belief in "social atoms on a footing of equality with one another" and "in universal laws of nature by which these atoms were combined," but posited the conception of "personalities constantly moving to different specific forms."[1] This led to a different notion of humanity. As Troeltsch observes: "Instead of ideas of the equal dignity of Reason everywhere, and of the fulfillment of universal law, we have the conception of a purely personal and unique realization of the capacities of Mind in every

[1] For notes to chap. iii, see pp. 131–132.

direction, primarily in individual persons, but secondarily also in communities themselves."[2] Intuition and emotion assumed greater importance than reason. In fact, the Romantic theory of knowledge was based upon intuition.

The state was conceived to have a spiritual essence, the product not of "contract and rationally purposive construction" but rather of "super-personal spiritual forces."[3] For eighteenth-century natural law, Romanticism substituted the *Volksgeist*. This was relative to time and place, but it was transcendent. The tendency was to deify the state, and, as Troeltsch says, to deify "the actual particular State."[4]

This way of thinking stimulated men to study history in order to discover the essential elements of the particular *Volksgeist*. It led to the founding of a historical school of jurisprudence (about 1809) which accepted as its motto Savigny's phrase that: *Das Gesetz ist das Organ des Volksrechts*. Henceforth nineteenth-century German jurisprudence, however it may have repudiated the historical school, accepted as axiomatic that law is relative in content to time and place. Moreover, as the study of history gradually endeavored to separate itself from philosophy, historiography was turned "into the paths of materialism or complete relativity."[5] The change in thought led in time to positivism; although at first, because of its intimate connection with philosophy, it was immersed in metaphysics.

Another impetus to the study of history came from science. Since the principle of causation in which scientific methodology was rooted had aided the natural scientist in deriving principles from the observation of successive physical events, the application of a similar idea of causation to the study of history seemed likely to yield comparable results. As scientific thought became dominant, as men sought to apply scientific analysis to human phenomena, men began to ask "how" more frequently than they asked "why." The experimental method based on empiricism and the inductive logic inherited from Aristotle and Bacon were the tools with which the scientist sought to examine the operation of the universe. Premised upon the belief that the universe is a rational whole, in the sense that it can be rationally understood, and that "every detailed occurrence can be correlated with its antecedents in a perfectly definite manner, exemplifying general principles,"[6] nineteenth-century science led men to believe that by empirical methods they could discover "positive facts" and "universal laws" about all phenomena, human as well as physical. Endeavoring to repudiate the search for "final causes," the scientist tried to content himself with the "pure" description of empirically observable "facts."

With increasing emphasis upon empiricism, less and less attention was given to metaphysical problems. In fact, the scientist thought that he had eliminated metaphysical problems, and, along with them, all questions of value judgment. Accordingly, as the physical scientist eliminated good and bad, beautiful and ugly, from his vocabulary, so did the student of human phenomena who accepted the scientific methodology. As a consequence, or perhaps as a corollary, philosophers themselves concentrated less attention on metaphysics and more upon epistemology. The question of *how* men know things became prior to the question of *what* they know.

The effect of this trend toward positivism, which culminated in the latter half of the nineteenth century, was to destroy all belief in transcendental truths and values. Judgments of right and wrong, good and bad, justice and injustice, were thought to be based upon utility or expediency. Value judgments were thought to be expressions of subjective preference rather than of objective truth. As materialism replaced pantheism and as empiricism stimulated subjectivism, conscience was denied a "scientifically" valid role in the determination of truth or value. Reasonable (logical) inductions from empirical "facts" supplanted right reason. Quantitative thinking became dominant.

Another consequence of the rejection of metaphysics and transcendent truth was the abandonment of the idea of natural rights peculiar to individuals as human beings. The scientist could not see a "soul"; he could not demonstrate empirically the absolute moral worth of individuals. Individual rights, therefore, could no longer be conceived transcendentally. Rights tended, accordingly, to be equated with interests. They were no longer regarded as existing prior to the state but rather as a consequence of the existence of the state. Rights were made dependent upon membership in a political community. In other words, individuals were no longer conceived as having rights as human beings but as citizens; for natural rights the nineteenth century substituted legal rights.

As a further result of the rejection of transcendent truth a change took place in the meaning of law. Law was conceived more and more as a product of will, of social forces, and less and less as an ideal standard. With the content of law, that is, transcendental truth, eliminated as the criterion of law, nothing remained but form. Scientific "'natural law' in the sense of 'the observed order of phenomenon' . . . tended . . . to crowd the earlier rationalistic conception to the wall, thus aiding the triumph of the idea of human and governmental law as an expression solely of will backed by force."[7] Substantive limitation to governmental authority, in the form of concrete individual rights, is abandoned. For, with the notion that the will of the law-making body needs only sufficient force behind it to make its will law, the only limitation is that the content of its will take the *form* of law. But it is a form ready for any content, indeed, even for content that might destroy individual rights and freedom.

In democratic countries, where this notion of positive law as the sole law was adopted along with the notion of the sovereignty of the legislative assembly, "all the varied rights of man were threatened with submergence in a single right, that of belonging to a popular majority, or more accurately, of being represented by a legislative majority."[8] Quantitative thinking triumphed. But there was no assurance that the will of the majority, popular or legislative, would always be right or just, unless the determination of rightness and justness was thought to be simply a matter of counting heads. What happened was that rightness and justness were abandoned as criteria of law; procedure and the manner of enactment, the source rather than the content of law, were substituted for justice as criteria of law.

To the will of the majority there was conceived to be no substantive limitation and whatever the majority enacted according to prescribed procedure was regarded as law. The legislative assembly might decide, indeed, as the German *Reichstag* did in 1933, to legislate itself out of existence in order that individuals might have the right of being "represented" by a "leader" who "knew" their desires better than did the *Reichstag* itself. Only a change in the conception of representation was necessary to make this a valid conclusion from the premises, and this change was not difficult to bring about—for if representation by a legislative majority is regarded simply as a technical device with no inherent claim to rightness or justness, representation by one man (claiming for himself seer-like powers) is *logically* just as valid a technical device. He can claim, with equal logical justification, to represent the will of the people. Then, whatever he enacts in the form of law backed by sufficient force must be regarded as law. His will, rather than the will of a legislative majority, fills in the content of law, but if the rightness and justice of the content of law have been eliminated as valid criteria of law, the possibility of evaluating his actions on these grounds has been eliminated at the same time.

The notion that law "is nothing but a standard of normalcy to regulate the universal service to the common interest"[9] does not preclude the possibility that one man may claim with equal logical validity to represent this "common interest" better than a legislative majority. Both agencies of representation may be regarded simply as technical devices, neither of which can lay claim to the inherent rightness or justness of the content of its will. As Ashton says, democrats are prone to think that the rule of the majority will provide "absolute justice—though in fact, of course, it is nothing but the subjective justice of a mass of democratic individuals."[10] Further he observes:

We cherish it as an ideal—although we know perfectly well that even in theory it can never be anything but the expression of what a particular group of human beings feels to be 'right' at a particular time. Now this is exactly what the Fascists maintain also. But they refuse to pursue even as an ideal the illusion of a justice independent from the group administering it. . . . Its justice is avowedly a subjective justice based upon communal interest.[11]

In essence, a principle of obligation, a *Sollen*, cannot be derived from a conception of law as simply the expression of will backed by force.

It is clear, at any rate, that the original concepts of liberalism became formalized to the extent that men accepted the perspective and premises of positivism. When men imbued with empiricism no longer believed in transcendental truth and value discoverable by reason, all objective limitation to will was removed. For, as Berdyaev rightly points out, "Freedom means not only freedom of choice, but choice itself."[12] As he says in another place: "Dynamic liberty is not formal freedom of choice; dynamic liberty presupposes a previous choosing of the truth."[13] It is not enough that men reason but that they reason from premises which they accept as true. Parliamentary institutions can only function effectively so long as minority as well as majority accept the same premises. These premises, moreover, cannot be reasoned about but must be accepted on faith. It is not enough, then, that men act reasonably; they must affirm certain truths and values in common.[14]

When men deny conscience a valid role in the scheme of things, in an attempt perhaps to be "scientific," freedom as conceived integrally degenerates into license. The link between subjective will and objective truth is destroyed. Law comes to be synonymous with command, its obligation resting no longer upon the justice of its content but upon the force that sanctions it. Law becomes at best a form ready to be filled in with any content, however just or unjust, good or bad.

This change in viewpoint, however, came about gradually. The philosophical school of thought was still dominant in the early nineteenth century, and the early historical school, so long as it maintained its connection with the philosophical school, was still integrally liberal. In place of the eighteenth-century concept of law as universal, eternal, absolute, and immutable, the historical school of the nineteenth century substituted the concept of law as relative to time and place. The legal order of the eighteenth century was grounded in "the nature of things" or in "human nature," but the legal order of the early nineteenth century was grounded in "history."

Law as Volksrecht

The historical jurist agreed with the eighteenth-century jurist that law is found and not made, but he looked for it in history and not in human nature. He was more of an empiricist than his predecessors but he did not rely upon empiricism alone. He found ideas of freedom and of justice evolving in history, and in this his thought was intimately related to that of the philosophical school of jurisprudence. Like the eighteenth-century jurist he believed in transcendental truths which limited arbitrary will. As Pound describes the historical school:

It did not think of a law which had always been the same but of a law which had grown. It sought stability through establishment of principles of growth, finding the lines along which growth had proceeded and would continue to proceed, and it sought to unify stability and change by a combination of historical authority and philosophical history. Utilizing the idea of authority, it sought to put a historical foundation under the seventeenth- and eighteenth-century theory of law as only declaratory of something having a higher authority than the pronouncement of legislator or judge as such. Law was not declaratory of morals or of the nature of man as a moral entity or reasoning creature. It was declaratory of principles of progress discovered by human experience of administering justice and of human experience of intercourse in civilized society; and these principles were not principles of natural law revealed by reason, they were realizings of an idea, unfolding in human experience and in the development of institutions—an idea to be demonstrated metaphysically and verified by history. All of this body of doctrine did not develop at once. But such was the creed of the school which was dominant in the science of law throughout the century and in one form or another this creed may be identified in all the varieties of juristic thinking during the century, even in schools which professed a different method.[15]

The historical school, particularly as it developed later on, was permeated with the idea of evolution. It was mechanistic in its attitude and tended to regard the universe as a great machine that ran by itself. Thus the historical school and its branches were opposed to reform and to legislation generally. As Pound says: "They conceived of a slow and ordered succession of events and of institutions whereby things perfected themselves by evolving to the limit of their idea."[16] Historical jurisprudence was deterministic and fatalistic. For although it apparently took account of growth and progress it falsely assumed that "it had discovered finally the immutable lines of growth or had calculated once for all the fixed orbit of progress outside of which no movement could possibly take place."[17]

It provided, however, the security and certainty that the bourgeoisie of the nineteenth century wanted most. The idea of equality, in the nineteenth century, meant "equality of operation of legal rules and equality of opportunity to exercise one's will and substance."[18] Security meant that "everyone is secured in his interests against aggression by others and others are to be permitted to acquire from him or to exact from him only through his will that they do so or through his breach of rules devised to secure others in like interests."[19] Thus, a formal rather than a substantive equality is espoused, and the end of law is no longer to provide justice but to provide security and the maximum possible individual self-assertion.

The law-of-nature school believed that the jurist by reason alone, without knowledge of the historical past, could frame a perfect and complete code. The jurist's task was simply to find the principles and the task of the legislator was to codify them. The judge was conceived to have no creative function; his task was simply to apply the code literally to the particular case.

The nineteenth century reacted against this optimistic rationalism and for a time there was some skepticism among jurists as to the possibility of legislating at all. This, at any rate, was the reaction of Savigny, for whom all law was the product of the folk mind or folk spirit. As he stated it: "all law is originally formed in the manner in which, in ordinary but not quite correct language, customary law is said to have been formed, *i. e.,* that it is first developed by custom and popular faith, next by jurisprudence—everywhere, therefore, by internal silently operating powers, not by the arbitrary will of the law-giver."[20]

He regarded law essentially as *Volksrecht,* as a product of the *Volksgeist.* This opinion was in keeping with the Romantic movement. Just as Arnim and Brentano found the embodiment of the folk spirit in popular songs, as the brothers Grimm found it in fairy tales and in language, so Savigny found the folk spirit embodied in law. Some of his followers were able to turn this idea of a folk spirit into a rampant nationalism but Savigny himself did not do so. A Romanist, rather than a Germanist, his conception of law as the product of the folk spirit was not in itself nationalistic.

However, the historical school, as represented by Savigny, relied upon the collective conscience of the folk community, expressed in customs and prevailing *mores,* as the sanction behind law. The natural-law school had relied upon the intrinsic justice of the rule and upon individual conscience as the sanction. Here, however, there is some difference. The idea that the sanction of law is the social pressure behind it led in time to the analytical conception that the sanction of law is the force supplied by the state. The historical school did not, of course, go so far, but it contained the germ of this idea. So long as the historical school maintained its intimate connection with metaphysics, this idea did not emerge, but when the historical school severed itself from the philosophical school the way was open for just such a conception of law.

Savigny regarded the character and content of law as fixed permanently in particular peoples. "In the earliest times to which authentic history extends," he wrote, "the law will be found to have already attained a fixed character, peculiar to the people, like their language, manners and constitution. . . . . That which binds them into one whole is the common conviction of the people, the kindred consciousness of an inward necessity, excluding all notion of an accidental and arbitrary origin."[21] Though Savigny saw growth and development in the past he assumed the essential datum as given from the beginning. He believed, as Korkunov points out, that:

... each people at its appearance on the arena of history had already its popular genius definitely established and containing in itself all the historic life of the people. In other words, this school comprehended the historic development as an organic and not a progressive one, not as an evolution. This was not meant to affirm that the development of law is the creation of some new factor, but only that it is the production of what from the beginning was already in embryo in the popular genius.[22]

This interpretation of legal history might be called, as it is by Pound, an ethical interpretation. It looks back into history and finds evidence to support the claim that history is nothing but the gradual unfolding or development of the idea of right or justice. The metaphysical basis for this interpretation was supplied by Kant. According to Kant "every action is right which in itself, or in the maxim on which it proceeds, is such that it can co-exist along with the freedom of will of each and all in action, according to a universal law."[23] One should act, therefore, so that the maxim of the act might be made a universal principle. One should treat each individual as an end and never as a means. It is reason that points out the duty of following the categorical imperative and the action to be followed. Kant discards eighteenth-century natural law and substitutes a different concept of justice, for, as Pound points out, "while to the eighteenth century justice meant the securing of absolute, eternal, universal rights of individuals, Kant held that it meant securing freedom of will to everyone so far as consistent with all other wills."[24]

By adopting in substance, although with some modification, Rousseau's concept of a general will, Kant succeeded in using this as the means by which individual wills within a state were reconciled. The state was founded he thought not by human will but by the reason immanent in human will. Freedom, thus, is not destroyed by membership in the state but actually so secured. The state is not based on utility but on the idea of freedom.

The early historical school of jurisprudence merged Kant's idea of a transcendent universal principle with an idealistic interpretation of history. Both the philosophical and the historical schools

. . . postulated an ideal law. One sought to discover this ideal law through history, the other sought to find it through logical development of an abstract idea. . . . Philosopher and historian were agreed that law was found, not made. One found it by deduction from a metaphysical principle, the other found it by historical study. Each, one need not say, found an ideal development of the principles of existing law; the historian because he so interpreted history, the philosopher because he was seldom a lawyer and got his facts and illustrations from the historian.[25]

Each school supplemented the other. From metaphysical deductions one found the form of law, from history and experience the content of law. So long as law was conceived to have both form and content, so long as the philosophical and historical schools supplemented one another, the conception of law was integrally liberal. But since Kant believed "that instead of eternal precepts of actual law there were but eternal principles of making law by which the actual precepts might be criticized"[26] Kant's theory, once it was divorced from the historical school, could easily lead to a sterile formalism.

There is a tendency here in Kant to make individual freedom possible only by membership in the state. It is an idea carried further by Hegel, who declares that there is no freedom outside the state. In a similiar vein, Puchta declared that "the Rights of Peoples are different; and the peculiar characteristics of a nation are exhibited in its System of Right, just as its Language and Customs."[27] Implicit in this statement of Puchta's is the idea that rights are not peculiar to individuals as human beings but peculiar to them as members of a particular folk community. Although Puchta did not go so far, it is but a short step to saying that rights are dependent upon the state for recognition and that they represent a concession by the state, a concession to be granted or refused. The direction in which these ideas point is brought out even more clearly when Puchta discusses the source of right. He wrote:

Through this common consciousness of Right, as by a common Language and a common Religion, the members of a people are bound together by a definite union. This union rests upon a certain relationship of body and mind; it extends beyond the intimacy of the inner family bond, and arises out of an actual division of the race of mankind. The consciousness which permeates the members of a people in common, is born with them and makes them spiritually members of one whole. It constitutes in a word, the national mind or spirit of the people; and it is the source of human or natural Right, and of the convictions of Right which stir and operate in the minds of individuals.[28]

In this kind of thinking, represented by the early historical school, the notion of the group or community tends to emerge as more important than the individual. The group, moreover, is not conceived as a plurality of individuals but as an entity and organism. The concept of social process supplied by the historical school "thrust into the foreground of the philosophic consciousness the notion of society as a developing organism achieving its continuity through some sort of selective process related to the performance of function."[29]

THE STATE AS THE PRODUCT OF ORGANIC GROWTH

This idea of society as an organic whole finds classic expression in Hegel. It was largely due to him that state and society were conceptually severed. Where former political thinkers had set the individual and the state over against one another, Hegel introduced the concept of society between the two, and it thus became possible to conceive of a science of the state as apart from a science of society. This concept of society, linked with the idea of evolution, made possible the later studies of Comte, Spencer and Marx.

Hegel himself had a concept of evolution and his "theory of organic unity was combined with a theory of historical dialectic which emphasized the continuity of history."[30] He tried to merge an a priori rationalism with historic realism but the result was not a genuine evolutionary theory, history was only the gradual unfolding of an idea, an idea that was assumed to start with. It did lay the basis, however, for further historical studies.

At any rate the introduction of the concept of society made it possible for Hegel to separate state and society and to personify the state, to give it a meaning that it had not had earlier. For the eighteenth century the state was something consciously created by individuals for individual purposes. For Hegel the state was not a contractual instrument, nor a creation of individual will, but an organ of the entire community fulfilling ends common to the community. It was the realization of an idea, an historic and logical necessity.

The state for Hegel is something real; it does not depend upon the will of individuals for its existence but is the product of organic growth. It is a person in the sense that it "has its basis and cause in itself."[31] It is a subject of rights and hence a juristic person. The concrete bearer of the state's personality is the monarch although the monarch is not identical with the state. For, "when the monarch says 'I will,' to legislative or executive proposals which are presented to him for approval, the State says 'I will' through him, but this, far from signifying that his will is the State's will, indicates rather that, although there can be no State will without him, he merely gives the subjective conative form to an already determined content."[32] Apart from his entire philosophical system, this concept would lead to uncontrolled absolutism, but for Hegel the content of action was predetermined in history and so was not arbitrary.

Since he believed that the real is rational and the rational is real and that development necessarily follows a dialectical process, he believed that the content of action was to be found in process and not in will. As an absolute idealist, he thought that this process was concerned with ideas, but Marx, using the same method but substituting economic forces for ideas, reached the same conclusion that the content of action is predetermined in the process. What Marx found predetermined was something quite different from what Hegel found, but the method was the same.

Throughout the greater part of the nineteenth century this notion of society evolving towards a certain predetermined end was dominant. The end was thought to be dictated by reason and verified by history. The process was thought to be inevitable, irreversible, and independent of individual will or desire. The limitation imposed upon arbitrary will was conceived to be "the spirit of history," the *Volksgeist,* or customs. Men believed that the less legislation there was the better. It was better to let the historical process work itself out unaided.

The dominant tone of the period was optimistic. As Whitehead observes: "The political, liberal faith of the nineteenth century was a compromise between the individualistic, competitive doctrine of strife and the optimistic doctrine of harmony. It was believed that the laws of the Universe were such that the strife of individuals issued in the progressive realization of a harmonious society. In this way, it was possible to cherish the emotional belief in the Brotherhood of Man, while engaging in relentless competition with all individual men."[33] The practical consequences of the doctrine of competition, the effects of the industrial revolution, particularly the creation of an industrial proletariat, did not bear out the optimism of the early nineteenth century. Theoretically, too, the Stoic-Christian idea of the Brotherhood of Man was undermined by the doctrine of evolution.

Darwin's doctrine of natural selection, when applied to human relations, emphasized strife rather than coöperation and "instead of dwelling on the brotherhood of man" emphasized "the extermination of the unfit."[34] The destruction of men is conceived as the "engine of progress."[35] With the gradual abandonment of Lamarck's doctrine that acquired characteristics can be transmitted from generation to generation and that in this way society may become progressively better, "progress" was conceived more and more as mechanical and was held to depend less and less upon individual effort. The implications of Malthus's doctrine, namely, that the poverty of the masses must be regarded as inevitable and that nothing can be done about it, made reform appear not only illusory but impossible.

Thus, when the philosophical jurists, aided by historical jurisprudence, declared that law is found and not made, and opposed legislation, they were reflecting a mentality that was buttressed by "science." By first accepting certain a priori premises and then examining history, they came to the conclusion that the present law was the product of the past, the unfolding of an idea of right or freedom. There was nothing anyone could do but accept the existing law as it was. They were not so much interested in the content of law as in the source of law. By regarding the content of law as fixed from the beginning, by regarding the growth of law as the filling in of details, as the logical or historical development of a given idea, they supplemented and gave affirmation to the ideas of Darwin, Malthus, and Spencer. Reform was impossible.

But implicit in the thought of the philosophical jurists were ideas which other men might use to refute them. While they asserted that law was found and not made, they regarded law as the product of the community, as peculiar to time and place. If law was the product of the community and if it was peculiar to time and place, then it might be regarded as a social instrument. Moreover, if society could change in character, one might assume that the content of law might also change. Moreover, they regarded the sanction of law as residing in the common "convictions" or "consciousness" of the people, and this might be taken to imply that a law which did not satisfy the wants and desires of the people was not really law at all.

Law as a Means to an End

In part, then, as a reaction to the philosophical and historical school, and in part as a result of the method which they employed, a new school of jurists arose to posit law as a means to an end rather than as an end in itself; these were the utilitarians. The shift in emphasis from the normative to the explanatory, already observable in the historical school, is carried further by the utilitarians. With the shift in emphasis from the philosophical to the empirical, the concept of society underwent a change. It became, as Talcott Parsons points out,

. . . the mechanism whereby individual wants, conceived to vary at random with no common standard, could be satisfied in the greatest possible degree under the existing conditions of human life. Social relations were thus reduced to the level of means to individual satisfactions. All idea of essentially normative control was abandoned; but on the other hand an element of determinism of a different sort was introduced by the analysis of the nature and extent of the limitations imposed by the conditions, the external environment and man's inherited nature under which it took place. Pushed to its final logical conclusion this determinism in terms of conditions ended up in the positivism of the later nineteenth century, completely eliminating the relativism of the earlier utilitarianism.[36]

Although the point of view of the utilitarian found classic expression in Bentham, it had a German representative in von Jhering, who was less extreme but who believed that "purpose is the creator of the entire law; that there is no legal rule which does not owe its origin to a purpose, *i.e.*, to a practical motive."[37] He recognizes coercion as the criterion of law and declares that "only those rules laid down by society deserve the name of law which have coercion, or since, as we have seen, the state possesses the monopoly of coercion, which have political coercion behind them:

whereby it is implicitly said that only the rules which are provided by the state with this efficacy are rules of law; or that *the state is the only source of law.*"[38] Thus it is the enforcement of a rule by the state that distinguishes it as law. "Law," he writes, "is the sum of the conditions of social life in the widest sense of the term, as secured by the power of the State through the means of external compulsion."[39] But it is not the physical force of the state alone which insures obedience to its law. There are certain psychological reasons why men support the state, namely: "insight into the necessity of political order; the sense of right and law; anxiety for the danger threatening persons and property in every disturbance of order; and fear of punishment."[40]

Von Jhering thinks that "there is a *social* mechanics to compel the human will just as there is a *physical* mechanics to force the machine. This social mechanics is identical with the principle of leverage, by means of which society sets the will in motion for her purposes, or in short, *the principles of the levers of social motion.*"[41] There are, he believes, four such levers, reward, coercion, the feeling of duty, and love[42]—the first two based upon egoism, and the latter two on universal ethical purposes. Thus he compromises between extreme utilitarianism and idealism. His whole theory is oriented around society rather than around the individual. "Securing the good of the individual," he says, "is not an end in itself, it is only a means to the end of securing the good of society."[43] The end of law, for von Jhering, is the satisfaction of human desires, interests, and claims, and it is "nature herself that has shown man' the way he must follow in order to gain another for his purposes: it is that of *connecting one's own purpose with the other man's interest.*"[44] Rights, in this view, tend to become equated with interests. In the thought of von Jhering the foundations were laid upon which an analytical school of jurisprudence might be based: he regarded law essentially as *made* and not found, and he distinguished law by the coercive force of the state behind it. Although the historical jurists had contended that law is discovered and not made, they had implied that law is the product of the community and peculiar in content to particular communities—in a sense, then, an instrument of communal life. At any rate this reading of history was as logical as theirs, once one began to examine history without assuming beforehand that it would demonstrate the gradual unfolding of an idea of right or freedom. Historical jurisprudence set in motion, therefore, a method of examination which in time was used to "prove" false the premises from which the historical jurists started.

THE EMERGENCE OF POSITIVISM

These tendencies latent in the various early nineteenth-century schools of jurisprudence culminated in the latter half of the century in positivism. With the emergence of the doctrine of evolution and the separation of history and philosophy, the "scientific" examination of history led men to believe that social groups exhibit the same phenomenon of growth as biological organisms, and obey similar principles of development. At first it was thought that the end of evolution was predetermined, that evolution was purposive and teleological. As science undermined metaphysical speculation, however, men were forced to examine their environment empirically and psychologically, and it was this reaction against rationalism and metaphysics that produced von Jhering and the utilitarians. In examining the legal system of their time, neglecting the historical approach, they found interest behind rights, psychological motivation and purpose. But the extreme subjectivism and relativism of utilitarianism produced a counter reaction.

Men wanted to preserve the empirical method given impetus by the historical school and the utilitarians, but they wanted, also, some objective order. The need felt by the dominant bourgeoisie for security, stability, and certainty demanded it. Since it was science which had largely undermined the metaphysical perspective, it was natural that men should turn to science for a new explanation. Since science, with its underlying philosophy of materialism, inspired men to regard man essentially as a biological organism obeying the physical laws that operated upon all matter throughout the universe, it was natural for men to believe that their institutions might be conceived as obeying similar laws of causation. An objective order independent of will could be conceived, accordingly, as embodied in this principle of physical causation, of natural compulsion. Such an order, moreover, could be regarded as functioning automatically. It was calculable (or so men thought), certain, and stable. It required neither will nor reason for its realization. Just as the physical scientist thought that this order was characterized by the competition of atoms issuing finally into harmony, so the social scientist thought it was characterized by the competition of individuals issuing finally in harmony. To achieve this harmony, however, one should let things run their course and let the "natural laws" operate without help or hindrance from human agencies. This was not the eighteenth-century natural order, which required will and the rational recognition of transcendent truth for its realization, but rather a natural order which, based upon sheer physical causation and compulsion, required neither will nor reason.

Positivism, then, is "a philosophical tendency oriented around natural science and striving for a unified view of the world of phenomena, both physical and human, through the application of the methods and the extension of the results whereby the natural sciences have attained their unrivaled position in the modern world."[45] It represents the victory of the empirical method and "calls 'positive' the facts and things of immediate perception as well as the relations and uniformities which thought may discover without transcending experience."[46] It regards as metaphysical "every inquiry which claims to go beyond the sphere of the empirical and seeks either hidden essences behind phenomenal appearances, or ultimate efficient and final causes behind things, as well as any attempt to attribute reality to species, ideas, concepts or the mind's logical 'intentions' in general."[47] It may be pointed out that the positivist does, in fact, engage in metaphysical speculation and that he assumes premises which are essentially beyond empirical proof or demonstration,[48] but it is equally significant that he denies this and acts as though it were not so.

According to the positivist doctrine "a Law of Nature is merely an observed persistence of pattern in the observed succession of natural things: Law is then merely Description."[49] It presupposes that "facts" may be directly observed and described without recourse to any scheme of values and equates understanding with description. "Its aim is to confine itself to fact, with a discard of all speculation."[50] Positivism sees no purpose in the universe but simply chance. As Whitehead observes, the world as the positivist sees it "exhibits . . . an involution of paths and a concatenation of circumstances which have arisen entirely by chance. We can describe what has happened, but with that description all possibility of knowledge ends."[51] Kant had already anticipated this conclusion for he had said that one could never know the ultimate nature of things, the *Ding-an-sich*. Consciousness, he thought, is restricted to the world of phenomena; it cannot invade the realm of the noumena. He did not adhere strictly to this in his ethical doctrines but his followers adhered to his positivist views long after they had abandoned his ethics.

One of the first, however, to give definite statement to the philosophy of positivism was Auguste Comte (1798–1857), who was also one of the first to establish sociology as a separate science. This was no coincidence for the two are mutually dependent, and arise from the same premises. In his *Cours de philosophie positive*, Comte outlines the three evolutionary stages through which he believes science and society have passed: the theological, the metaphysical, and the positive.[52] In the theological stage, he says, imagination plays the principal role and man interprets his environment in terms of gods and spirits. At the metaphysical stage universal ideas or energies are used to explain the universe and here the idea of nature is substituted for the idea of God. The third stage, the positive, subordinates both imagination and reflection to experience. Truth is said to consist of "empirical facts." And by observing the succession of these facts one is able inductively to find certain laws of relationship. He divided the sciences into mathematics, astronomy, physics, chemistry, biology, and sociology. The latter is a "social physics" and its task is to discover the "laws" that govern social life. By conceiving of society as an organism and by applying the scientific notion of cause and effect to its development, Comte thought he could explain its evolution mechanically and logically.

The implication of positivism, as carried further by the followers of Comte, is that social phenomena, like all natural and physical phenomena, can be studied by the scientific method, and that human phenomena, like physical phenomena, obey certain laws of nature which can be inductively discovered by examining a succession of events empirically. These laws do not transcend experience, according to the positivist, but are found immanently in things themselves, and behind them is the compulsion of nature, which, independent of individual will or desire determines the course of events. And just as the physical scientist finds compulsion behind physical law so the positive jurist finds compulsion behind governmental law. For both it is compulsion that is the criterion of law. Just as there is no place for value judgments in physical science so there is no place for value judgments in social science; as the physical scientist is unconcerned with the ethical or aesthetic implications of conclusions arrived at by an "objective analysis" of empirical "facts," so the social scientist is unconcerned with the good or bad implications of the conclusions of his observations. The only task left to social science and jurisprudence is the description of events and the induction from these events of general laws of causality—the evaluation of the goodness or badness, the justice or injustice, of particular events being regarded as not only irrelevant scientifically but incompatible with the scientific method. With value judgments (apparently) eliminated, conscience is denied a valid role in the ascertainment of truth.

The effect of positivism upon legal thought will be dealt with in more detail later but certain generalizations can be made now. By rejecting everything that transcends experience, positivism undermines the idea of law as being filled with substantive content in the sense of eternal truths and values. It leads to a separation of will and norm, fact and standard, and destroys the *Bindung* and mutual dependency which will and norm had in integral liberalism. Standards can no longer be derived from facts nor facts from standards. Positivism severs finally the realm of the *Sein* from the realm of the *Sollen*. In consequence of this separation, toward the turn of the century, two schools of jurists arose: the Neo-Kantians who restricted themselves to the realm of the *Sollen* and rejected all substantive criteria of law and the Neo-Hegelians who restricted themselves to the realm of the *Sein* and rejected all normative criteria of law. The theories of the former school led to irresponsibility on the part of the individual and those of the latter to irresponsibility on the part of the state. In both the integral-liberal concept of freedom becomes degenerate.

CHAPTER IV

FORMAL LIBERALISM

The purely formal comprehension of liberty has led to actual non-liberty. . . . Liberty was discovered to be protection of the rights of the strong, leaving the weak defenceless.

—NICHOLAS BERDYAEV.

THE PROCESS OF FORMALIZATION

INTEGRAL LIBERALISM conceives of freedom as the opportunity for the individual, unrestrained by arbitrary or personal authority, to follow the dictates of conscience. The individual is free—not free to do anything he pleases—but free from any will that is arbitrary or capricious. He is free under the law, under the impersonal authority of a law that transcends individuals and whose content is discoverable by right reason. Integral liberalism assumes that individuals will reason from the same premises within a framework of values acknowledged by all. It is conscience that recognizes and embodies these values and conscience that bids the individual to reason rightly, to reason objectively. Thus it is conscience that links the transcendent, potential, objective order with individual, subjective will. The common recognition of certain eternal truths and values links will and norm, fact and standard, inseparably together.

Liberalism, as integrally conceived, takes as its fundamental premise the absolute value of human personality. This is regarded as an eternal truth. Since the individual is a moral entity, equal in moral worth with every other individual, he has certain rights and responsibilities by virtue simply of his humanity. Each individual is obligated not only to seek his own freedom but the freedom of every other individual. For, without freedom for all there can be no freedom (in the integral-liberal sense of the word) for any individual. If the rights of each individual are not respected there is no assurance that the rights of any individual will be protected. Each individual is obligated, therefore, to guarantee the rights of every other individual, rights which are not peculiar to individuals as citizens but as human beings.

In the nineteenth century, however, particularly in the latter

[70]

half of the century, these original concepts of liberalism change. Freedom under the law is espoused by nineteenth-century liberals, but it differs altogether from its earlier meaning. The concept of individuality and the concept of law are altered. The claim which integral liberalism makes for individual dignity, autonomy, and responsibility rests, in the final analysis, upon the presupposition of the essential moral worth of human beings. This notion of the absolute moral value of human personality is undermined in the nineteenth century—in the first half of the century by Romanticism which emphasizes individual differences, and in the second half by the theory of evolution and the infiltration of positivism into all realms of thought. The existence of the individual soul cannot be empirically demonstrated and it is rejected as scientifically irrelevant, if not invalid. In place of the "soul" the scientist substitutes the "psyche," and a new science, psychology, a kind of mental physics, lends its authority to this change. The scientific principle of cause and effect is translated into behaviorist psychology in terms of stimulus and response. The "psyche" of the individual, like his body, is "explained" in terms of mechanical principles; mind is either equated with body or regarded as an epiphenomenon of body. If the latter half of the nineteenth century, as Tillich observes, neglects the soul, then it assiduously cultivates the body.[1] Sports, gymnastics, and physical culture are emphasized in an attempt "to achieve a unified development of the whole personality through physical development and discipline."[2]

If science aids men to abandon a belief in the essential spirituality of individuals, then capitalism abets this endeavor. "For the idea of the end of the world," nineteenth-century capitalist society "substituted the idea of progress."[3] Progress means, moreover, the progressive betterment of man's material status. The aim is simply to provide man with an increasingly better-furnished dwelling place, and this is regarded as an end in itself. With the growth of the capitalist system, profits are substituted for the values of human personality, and material values are made the measure of all things. Capitalism, as Tillich remarks, aims "to provide the greatest possible number of men with the greatest possible amount of economic goods," and "seeks to arouse and to satisfy ever-increasing demands without raising the question as to the meaning of the

---

[1] For notes to chap. iv, see pp. 133–134.

process which claims the service of all the spiritual and physical
human abilities."[4] Few question why men should have more and
more economic goods or the meaning of the eternal striving for
profits. Material comfort and the accumulation of wealth is a
self-sufficient end. As Tillich says: "In all of this there is no trace
of self-transcendence, of the hallowing of existence. The *forms* of
the life-process have become completely independent of the source
of life and its meaning. They are self-sufficient and produce a self-
sufficient present."[5] From an aspect and means of life, economic
activity becomes, in the nineteenth century, an end in itself. As
a result of the increasing dominance of economic activity in man's
thought and life, all other aims, social and political, are subordinated. The state's function becomes that of preserving the
system. It becomes completely secularized; the only task assigned
to it "is the legal protection of the economic life in internal and
external relations."[6]

As a consequence of its complete secularization, the state adopts
an attitude of indifference to things spiritual. It affirms nothing
spiritual; it is agnostic. Just as it allows individuals in the economic sphere to pursue their own interest in their own way, within
certain formal limitations, so it allows individuals in matters
spiritual to think, worship, and speak as they please. Anything can
be done, anything can be said, so long as it does not disturb the
existing economic order, and so long as it is done in conformity
with certain formal, procedural requirements. The *way* in which
a thing is done or said, *how* it is done, is the only consideration—
what is done or said is irrelevant. (For example, overthrow of the
existing order can be advocated so long as it does not actually lead
to violence.) By its agnosticism the state actually affirms spiritual
anarchy. Berdyaev has rightly called this the "age of sceptical
liberty."[7]

It should be emphasized that the liberalism of this age is not
integral liberalism; rather, it is a liberalism which retains the
forms of integral concepts but discards their content. It substitutes
economic for spiritual content, self-immanence for self-transcendence, a self-sufficient here and now for the promise of eternal
salvation. It substitutes spiritual agnosticism for tolerance within
a value system. For the idea of a "calling," it substitutes the accumulation of wealth, material comfort and pleasure. For the

asceticism of early capitalism, which was intimately related to Protestant theology,[8] it substitutes frank indulgence in worldly goods and pleasures.

FORMAL FREEDOM AND FORMAL EQUALITY

Since the nineteenth century rejects the notion of the absolute moral value of human personality it must necessarily reject the conclusions derived from this premise. Nineteenth-century liberals cling to the notions of equality and freedom but, since they reject the content supplied by the idea of the absolute moral worth of individuals, these concepts can be conceived only in a formal sense. It is formal liberty, they espouse, and formal equality. Nineteenth-century liberals speak of freedom and equality under the law, but they conceive of the law as drawing its content from individual wills and interests. Conscience no longer supplies the content of law because belief in eternal truths and values is discarded. Law is conceived as a rationally devised instrument for the attainment of certain social purposes. Hence, in the last analysis, the criterion of law can only be the force behind it. Expediency replaces rightness. It is the purpose for which men unite and voluntarily subject themselves to the might of the community that is regarded as the source of legal obligation, rather than the common recognition of the justness of the content of law. It is not the justness of a rule that determines the obligation to obey it but the compulsion behind it. The content of law is irrelevant, since only the form determines its legality.

Law is not prior to the state but the state is prior to the law. Since the criterion of law is coercion, rather than morality, the state, as the agency which possesses the most powerful instruments of coercion, is prior to law. Individual rights, moreover, become rights of citizens rather than rights of human beings. The protection of rights rests solely upon the state, since rights are divorced from moral responsibilities. Rights tend to become equated with interests, with interests, moreover, which have sufficient force behind them to compel recognition on the part of the weaker members of society. Integral liberalism conceives of individual rights as being rooted in the spirituality of individuals; formal liberalism thinks of them as social concessions—properly speaking not rights at all.

When the nineteenth-century liberal spoke of freedom and equality for individuals he meant freedom and equality for individuals as political units, not as human beings. As Berdyaev observes, this "emphasis upon man as a citizen covered and obscured the concept of man as a free spirit belonging to another order of being, and on the other hand it obstructed the vision of man as a labourer and producer."[9] The state protected legal rights, not human rights, and the rights of the individual were "confined to the formal and political sphere of his life and were not conceived as extending into the economic sphere."[10]

It was immaterial for the notion of law (as conceived by formal liberalism) whether one individual was stronger economically than another, whether one individual, by virtue of the economic power at his disposal, had greater actual freedom than another; the law protected the formal freedom and equality of each. It was not concerned with actual freedom or actual equality. The nineteenth-century state, as Anatole France has observed, "forbade in majestic equality the rich as well as the poor to steal bread and to beg on the street corners."[11] Freedom as conceived by integral liberalism consisted of substantive human rights; freedom, for the formal liberals, consisted simply of formal rights, and meant the securing of the rights of the stronger individuals. Thus, liberty turned out to be "the protection of the rights of a privileged minority, the defense of capitalistic property and the power of money."[12]

The liberals of the seventeenth and eighteenth centuries spoke of the protection of the rights of property, but they had a very different conception of property from that held by nineteenth-century liberals. They thought of property as an attribute of personality, and, while they acknowledged that property might be unequally (but not inequitably) distributed, they thought that each individual would have some. It was not corporate property they defended. "Yet," as Crane Brinton points out, "throughout the nineteenth century and into the twentieth, in the industrial countries, the doctrine of natural rights was used to defend a kind of property which in its extension, in its concentration in relatively few hands, in its very nature, was totally different from the property with which Locke and his followers were familiar."[13] Moreover, the seventeenth and eighteenth centuries, unlike the nineteenth, did not divorce rights from responsibilities.

When Adam Smith spoke of freedom he had a very different notion of freedom from that of nineteenth-century liberals. He wrote, for example:

Though every man may, according to the proverb, be the whole world to himself, to the rest of mankind, he is the most insignificant part of it. Though his own happiness may be of more importance to him than that of all the world besides, to every other person it is of no more consequence than that of any other man. [4]

And in another place:

The wise and virtuous man is, at all times, willing that his own private interest should be sacrificed to the public interest of his own particular order or society. He is, at all times, willing, too, that the interest of this order or society should be sacrificed to the greater interest of the state or sovereignty, of which it is only a subordinate part: he should, therefore, be equally willing that all those inferior interests should be sacrificed to the greater interest of the universe, to the interest of that great society of all sensible and intelligent beings, of which God himself is the immediate administrator and director.[15]

Above the positive law Smith recognized a higher law:

Every system of positive law may be regarded as a more or less imperfect attempt towards a system of natural jurisprudence, or *towards an enumeration of the particular rules of justice.* As the violation of justice is what men will never submit to from one another, the public magistrate is under a necessity of employing the power of the commonwealth to enforce the practice of this virtue. . . . To prevent the confusion which would attend upon every man's doing justice to himself, the magistrate, in all governments. . . . undertakes to do justice to all. . . . Sometimes what is called the constitution of the state, that is, the interest of the government; sometimes the interest of particular orders of men who tyrannize the government, warp the positive laws of the country from what natural justice would prescribe. . . . Grotius seems to have been the first to attempt to give the world anything like a system of those principles which ought to run through, and be the foundation of the laws of all nations.[16]

Integral liberals, like Adam Smith, believed that the state existed "to do justice to all." They recognized that men must make a constant and vigilant endeavor to bring positive law into conformity with the principles of natural justice. They regarded a positive law that served the particular interests of one group as "warped." In short, integral liberalism presupposed the existence of certain eternal, transcendent truths and values; by the end of the nineteenth century, with the infiltration of positivism into all realms of thought, this belief was abandoned. Presuppositions that had been regarded as self-evident in the seventeenth century were subjected by nineteenth-century positivism to a scrutiny that declared them to be highly doubtful and scientifically untenable.

INDUCTION SUPPLANTS RIGHT REASON

The positivist sociologists, particularly those influenced by Darwin, "sought for absolute mechanical social laws whose inevitable operations produced all social, political and jural institutions, as completely apart from human will as the motions of the planets."[17] For the transcendent order of the seventeenth and eighteenth centuries, which was realized by will guided by reason but was not dependent upon will for its existence, they substituted an immanent order which was neither dependent upon will for its existence nor realized by will. It was discoverable not by right reason but by inductive "scientific" methods.

Similarly, "the positivist jurists sought to find laws of morals and laws of legal and social evolution analagous to gravitation, conservation of energy and the like, and they expected to find these laws through observation and experience."[18] Where the historical jurist, in examining the development of law, "found metaphysical laws" behind this growth, "the mechanical sociologist found physical laws."[19] Both agreed that the content of law was given . To the historical jurist, however, the content was something transcendent, to the positivist jurist the content was something immanent. What was the result of this new view? Pound says:

The old natural law called for search for an eternal body of principles to which the positive law must be made to conform. This new natural law called for search for a body of rules governing legal development, to which law will conform do what we may. The operation of these same rules will change it and change it in accordance with fixed and definite rules in every way comparable to those which determine the events of nature. The most man may do is to observe and thus, it may be, learn to predict. For the rest nature will take her inexorable course and we may but impotently wring our hands. If law is an inevitable resultant, if in making it or finding it, legislator or judge is merely bringing about 'conformity to the *de facto* wishes of the dominant forces of the community,' conscious effort to improve the law can be effective in appearance only.[20]

The historical jurist denied that the legislator had any creative function. He "said that the law could no more be made than language. Each was a growth upon the basis of a received tradition."[21] The positivist jurist not only denied to the legislator any creative function but "added a doctrine of juristic futility."[22] Jurisprudence, too, became a formal science. Divorced from ethics and philosophy, it concerned itself simply with developed systems of law, with legal forms rather than legal contents. The question of what ought to be was no longer a valid or relevant problem for the jurist. He was concerned only with what was given, with positive law as he found it. This way of thinking, it should be observed, was quite different from the eighteenth-century notion, for, as Pound points out, even if the eighteenth-century theory "put the basis of legal systems beyond reach of change" it did urge men "to scan the details and to endeavor to make each part conform to the fixed ideal plan. It admitted that legislator and jurist each had a function."[23]

JURISPRUDENCE BECOMES A FORMAL SCIENCE

In Germany, jurisprudence was transformed into a formal science through the work of men like Gerber, Laband, and Jellinek. It is with them, that is, about 1870, that liberalism might fairly be said to decline. It is with them that will and norm, fact and standard, began to be separated so that at the turn of the century either one or the other had to be made absolute. And it was with this complete separation of fact and standard that liberalism became degenerate.

The study of law prior to Gerber had usually been included in what was called *allgemeine Staatslehre* or *Politik,* studies which also included political theory. With the introduction of the concept of society and the consequent development of sociology as a separate study, the study of law was divorced, for a time at least, from sociological considerations. Under the influence of positivism, moreover, the study of law was confined to an analytical examination of the existing body of positive law, so that under Gerber and those who followed him an attempt was made to establish a "science of law," a *Staatsrechtswissenschaft,* which would exclude general political considerations and political theory. It was to be a study of law as such without relation to general social or political problems, ends, or purposes. The new school of jurists accepted the law as they found it, they accepted the content of law as given and concerned themselves only with the formal analysis of the existing body of law.

Liberalism, in its integral form, merged, it will be recalled, two self-sufficient theories of obligation.[24] These were merged historically and without any conscious recognition of their mutual independence and inconsistency. Law was regarded as the product of individual consent but it was regarded also as the embodiment of eternal and absolute truths, secured transcendentally in the natural order. Man was obligated to obey law, according to the first theory, because it was to his own interest (expedient) to do so; he was obligated, according to the second theory, because he recognized through his conscience that the law embodied objective truth, eternal principles of justice. The historicism and positivism of the nineteenth century destroyed belief in eternal, transcendent, truths and values. Principles of justice were regarded as meta-juristic and, hence, irrelevant to a study of law that endeavored to be scientific. It was not content but form that distinguished law. Attention was focused upon procedure, on the way in which law was enacted, rather than upon what was enacted.

To integral liberals the "rule of law" was synonymous with the rule of just principles. To formal liberals the "rule of law" came to mean the automatic application of rules regardless of their content. For integral liberals the *Rechtsstaat* was a "state of rights" based upon justice to all; for formal liberals the *Rechtsstaat* was a state in which administrative discretion was reduced to a minimum; it was a state in which governmental law was applied as automatically and impersonally as the laws of nature. All substantive, objective limitations to will were removed; only formal, procedural limitations were left. Limitation could only be secured immanently and formally. Any limitation now must necessarily be self-limitation—or force!

Translated into political reality, this meant that there was no limitation, except that which was self-imposed, upon the law-making organs of the state. Equality and freedom under the law no longer meant substantial equality and equal freedom but equal application of the law whatever its content to all individuals. As Heller has expressed it, the notion of equality before the law became simply "a formal administrative maxim which demanded balanced application of law to the individual case without regard to the just or unjust content of the law . . . it was only a question of arithmetical application of the law, no longer of justice or rightness."[25] Thus the liberals of the latter part of the nineteenth century, men like Gerber, Jellinek, and Laband, still espoused freedom for the individual under the law but because of their concept of law, the freedom they espoused was a formal, technical freedom —no longer the substantive freedoms espoused by the liberals of the seventeenth and eighteenth centuries. Their conception of liberalism consequently might fairly be distinguished from integral liberalism by calling it formal liberalism.

THE STATE AS THE SOURCE OF LAW

Having denied that there was any other law than positive law, having denied that there was a transcendent order, the positivist liberal jurists were forced to conclude that the source of law is the state. They conceived of the state as a juristic person with a will of its own. Theoretically this subordinated the monarch to the rule of law, and by positing a state will they were able, abstractly at least, to distinguish the will of the state from the will of the monarch. As Gerber expressed it: "The State's power to will, political power, is the law of the State."[26] It was not individuals, he contended, who decided the content of will but the state as a juristic person. The will of the state was, in a sense, the will of all individuals united politically. The will of the state "ist das Herrschen, d.h. rechtliches Handeln im Interesse des Staatszweckes mit einer das ganze Volk verpflichtenden Wirkung."[27] There is an attempt here to retain an impersonal source of law.

Gerber admitted, however, that for practical purposes "the monarch formally absorbs the personality of the State into his own personality,"[28] but he insisted that the will of the state was a real, not a fictitious, will, that "this power to will is something existing in and for itself."[29] This distinction between the will of the monarch and the will of the state is a tenuous one, and for practical purposes they are essentially indistinguishable. To say, therefore, that the source of law is the will of the state as a juristic person, and to say at the same time that it is only made manifest through the will of the monarch, is to say, for practical purposes, that the source of law is the will of the monarch. Gerber did not carry the idea so far but this inference from his statement is logical.[30]

Gerber thought that the power of the state to will was limited by the ends which it pursued.[31] He thought for this reason that the state's power was not absolute but limited. The reasoning, however, is fallacious. Since, according to his theory, the state itself determines what ends it shall pursue, it also determines what it wills. Moreover, to say that will is limited by purpose is meaningless, for will without purpose is inconceivable. It is necessary to will something in order to will at all; willing implies choice and decision. The limitation which Gerber posits, therefore, is highly abstract and formal, and for all practical purposes is no limitation at all.

The fiction of the state as a juristic person, somehow apart from the governmental organs through which its will is made manifest, was accepted by Paul Laband. Only the state can enforce rules which are binding on individuals; it alone, says Laband, can demand compliance, suggest or prohibit action on the part of its citizens. This is the essential thing which distinguishes the state from other organizations and persons. Its rules or law, consequently, are the only law. The distinguishing aspect of law, moreover, is its binding force, its form, not its content. "The specific activity of the power of the State, its rulership," Laband declares, "appears not in the production of the content of law, but only in sanctioning the validity of law, in equipping a legal prescript with power to bind, with outer authority."[32]

The parliament may decide the content of law but it does not become law until it is sanctioned by the monarch. To Laband *"the sanction is the heart of the whole process of legislation;* everything that precedes it in the way of legislation is only preparation for it, fulfillment of necessary conditions; everything that follows it is necessary legal consequence of the sanction, unalterably brought about by it."[33] Zorn accepted Laband's theory but put it even more directly when he declared:

The sanction is that public law act which perfects the law. In the sanction lies the command in law. Whoever issues the command is the legislator. The sanction is the highest and true act of legislation; therefore the right of sanction belongs only to the bearer of sovereignty.[34]

The "bearer of sovereignty," of course, was conceived to be the state as a juristic person manifesting its will through the will of the monarch. For practical purposes, if not theoretical, the "bearer of sovereignty" and the "true" legislator, therefore, was not the parliament but the monarch. The parliament might determine the content of law but it was only binding if sanctioned by the sovereign, which for all practical purposes, meant the monarch.

It would seem from such a theory that the monarch was absolute, that the sovereign, at any rate, could will as he pleased. There would seem to be no limitation upon arbitrary or capricious action on the part of the sovereign. Some of the critics of Gerber and Laband pointed this out. The formal jurists replied, however, that this was not the case, that they did acknowledge that there was limitation—this being, in fact, their claim to the title of liberals. "The imperium in the modern civilized State," wrote Laband, "is no arbitrary power, but one determined by legal prescriptions. It is the characteristic of the *Rechtsstaat* that the State can require no performance and impose no restraint, can command its subjects in nothing and forbid them in nothing, except on the basis of a legal prescription."[35] Obviously, the whole crux of the matter rests upon the conception of "a legal prescription." Since, as shown above, Laband thought that "a legal prescript with power to bind" could only be issued by the state it follows that the only limitation upon the will of the state is the will of the state. In other words the only limitation is self-limitation.

Now so long as a theoretical distinction was made between the will of the state and the will of the monarch, Laband could say that the law which bound the state was independent of a personal will. But, even admitting this highly artificial and formal distinction, it is still difficult to see how self-limitation is actual limitation. If the distinguishing thing about law is the sanction behind it, who is to coerce the state into obedience, if conceivably, it fails to be bound by its own law? The answer is that only that which the state acknowledges to be law is law; hence, it cannot fail to be bound by its own law. This is reasoning in a circle but it is typical of the thought of "liberals" like Laband and Jellinek.

THE STATE CONCEIVED AS SELF-LIMITING

Since the state itself says what law is, the state can only be conceived as self-limiting. "It is not disputed," Laband wrote, "that there must be a supreme and highest power, which is subordinated to no other earthly power, and which is in truth the *potestas suprema*. The criterion of supreme and highest power exists in the fact that it is determined only by itself and can receive no legally binding prescriptions from any other power."[36] In similar vein Jellinek declared: " . . . a power to rule becomes legal by being limited. Law is legally limited power. The potential power of the community is greater than its actual power. Through auto-limitation it achieves the character of legal power."[37] When Jellinek says "law is legally limited power" he is simply saying law is limited by law—which means nothing. It seemed to mean something to the formal jurists, however, and his theory of auto-limitation won wide acceptance among German jurists.

Actually Jellinek implied that the power of the state is unlimited. Potentially at least, the state is omnipotent. It is a doctrine that foreshadows in many striking ways the doctrine of the National Socialists. He defined sovereignty as " . . . the exclusive capacity of the power of the State to give its ruling will a universally binding content, to determine its own legal order in every direction" and "the impossibility of being legally restrained by any other power against its own will."[38] The logical implication from this is that the state is potentially omnipotent. The state can make any content binding that it desires.

But Jellinek, irked by critics who contended that he made the state omnipotent, declared that sovereignty

is not State omnipotence. It is legal power and bound by the law. To be sure, it suffers no legal limits: the State can rid itself of every self-imposed limitation, but only within the *forms of law* and by creating new limits. *Not the individual limit but the fact of limitation is the permanent factor.* As little as the absolutely restricted State exists, so little does the State with absolutely boundless sovereignty.[39]

Now actually of course no state is omnipotent in the sense that it can do anything it pleases. The Fascist state recognizes certain self-imposed limitations. As one writer says, "Fascism could easily justify its absolutistic and antiliberal tendencies in the elaborations of the theory of auto-limitation so soon as it could assume the congruence of the Fascist party with the state, and of the state with the nation."[40] If the "fact of limitation" is sufficient criterion for the *Rechtsstaat,* then the Fascist state is a *Rechtsstaat.* It acknowledges no individual limitation to its power, it recognizes no substantive individual rights, but according to Jellinek this is not a necessary criterion of the *Rechtsstaat.* It was, however, for the integral liberal!

What Jellinek says, in effect, is that the legality of an action does not depend upon the content of the action but on the form of the action. Anything can be done if it is done according to a certain legal procedure. And even the procedure can be changed so long as some new procedure (any procedure) is substituted. The limitation he envisages is purely formal, technical, procedural. If the state acknowledges some limitation to its power it is a *Rechtsstaat*. This is quite a different notion from that espoused by Fichte. Fichte and Humboldt, as has been shown, recognized *substantive*, as well as formal, limitations upon the power of the state. Jellinek recognizes no substantive limitations. Jellinek contends that the legislative power of the state is bound only by formal, procedural limitations. In this sense it is under the law, but in no other sense. Such a theory, however much Jellinek may have doubted it—and he did—prepares the way for despotism; as a matter of fact, it makes it possible to legislate despotism into existence, just as the *Reichstag* eventually did in 1933. The legislature can legislate itself out of existence and adopt a new procedure that dispenses with its services.

If the state itself determines its own competency, the extent of its own power and the content of its own law, who is to say the state is wrong? By abolishing from jurisprudence all considerations of right and wrong, justice and injustice, Jellinek and the other formal jurists might consistently answer that the question is invalid and irrelevant. From their point of view it is irrelevant, from the point of view of an integral liberal it is not only a valid question but a crucial one. To the latter the *Rechtsstaat* is not simply a legal formula, nor a device to provide equal application of positive law (whatever its content) to every individual but it exists to provide substantial justice to each individual, justice in terms of a law that is higher and more binding than any positive law.

The notion of an impersonal rule of law which the formal jurists espoused was premised upon the concept of the state as a juristic person. Jellinek contended that this idea of the state as a juristic person was, indeed, an abstraction but not a fiction.[41] But he admitted that a state without organs was inconceivable—"Der staat kann nur durch das Medium von Organen walten; denkt man die Organe hinweg, so ist auch die Vorstellung des Staates selbst verschwunden."[42] In similar vein, Triepel declared that the organs *were* the state and that without them the state was nothing.[43] Haenel, too, contended that the state had no reality apart from its organs.[44]

The state, then, as conceived by the formal jurists, was an intellectual abstraction although its will was made manifest through its organs. The high abstraction and formality of their thinking is demonstrated by this kind of reasoning. The state, as a juristic person, as an intellectual abstraction, has a will but this will is only made manifest through its organs. Hence, for practical purposes, the will of the state and the will of its organs are indistinguishable. This comes very near to saying, if it does not actually acknowledge, that a command is law if it issues from an organ of the state. By positing the state as an abstraction with an abstract will behind the law, the formal liberals theoretically avoid saying this but for practical purposes there is no one able to distinguish the will of the state from the will of its organs. Their notion, then, of an impersonal rule of law rests upon casuistic reasoning.

INDIVIDUAL RIGHTS AS LEGAL RIGHTS

From the conception of law as a rule sanctioned by the state, as a manifestation of the will of the state, it follows that individual rights have to be conceived as legal rights, as concessions made by the state. According to liberalism in its integral form an individual has certain rights by virtue of his humanity; according to formal liberalism he has certain rights as a citizen, as a member of a legal community. As one writer has expressed it the theory of the formal jurists "proceeds not from the individual but from the State, whatever rights a person has he has not by virtue of being an individual but because the State itself sets certain auto-limitations to its power."[45]

There can be rights against the state only when the individual and the state are both subordinated to the same order of law. But when the state is conceived as the source of law, and hence above the law, there can be no rights against it. Individual rights can only be thought of as concessions granted by the state. If they are concessions they can, theoretically and practically, be granted or withdrawn, extended or limited, at will. They are not absolute rights, secured transcendentally, but relative rights, secured immanently in a particular legal system. Rights are no longer conceived of as being antecedent to the state but as depending upon the state for their existence. "Only as a member of the State," says Jellinek, " . . . is man the bearer of rights."[46] "Personality," in fact, he says, "is *iuris publici*."[47]

The slave, Jellinek contends, possessed no personality before he was freed by the state. As he puts it:

Der Sklave war, ehe der Staat ihn befreite oder doch in beschränktem Sinne als mit Verfügungsgewalt über sein peculium ausgerüstet anerkannte, nicht Person, auch nicht in dem Sinne, dass sie ihm als nicht zur Anerkennung gekommene Qualität anhaftete. Als Mensch war er natürlich anerkannt. Dies äusserte sich aber nur darin, dass er zwar nicht Rechtssubjekt, wohl aber Pflichtsubjekt war. *Aus dem Wesen des Menschen ergibt sich historisch und logisch als notwendig nur die Pflicht, aber nicht das Recht gegen den Staat.*[48]

If an individual has rights against the state, he has them, Jellinek contends, not by virtue of his humanity but by virtue of his legal personality, that is, as the member of a legal community. Rights rest upon status.

It is not correct, Jellinek says, to speak of individual liberties but only of individual liberty.[49] And what is this liberty or freedom? He answers: "Alle Freiheit is einfach Freiheit von *gesetzwidrigen* Zwange."[50] It is a significant characteristic of his thought that he uses *gesetzwidrig* rather than *rechtswidrig*. Freedom means freedom from all illegal compulsion, not necessarily, however, freedom from unjust compulsion. In other words, the individual cannot be commanded to do anything except by law, his freedom can be limited only by legal prescription. Individual freedom, therefore, is a formal not a substantive freedom; it is relative, not absolute. The dividing line between the sphere of state activity and the sphere of individual freedom is a purely formal not a material one.

If individual rights are to mean anything, there must be some way to guarantee them against arbitrary aggression on the part of the state. Jellinek contended that individual rights were secured by subordinating the executive to the law and by providing machinery by which the legality of administrative acts might be challenged by individuals.[51] Jellinek said that the executive could only command the individual when authorized by a legal prescription. Every act had to find its justification in law. He thought that the administrative courts of his time adequately provided opportunity for the individual to seek redress for any illegal adminis-trative acts. It is a formal guarantee which he provides and not a substantial one.

COMPULSION AS CRITERION OF LAW

Jellinek and the other formal jurists do not deny that there are social, psychological, and moral checks to state power, but as jurists they are not concerned with these. They admit that there are cultural and moral forces behind the law, but as jurists they rec-ognize only the sanction behind the law as its distinguishing fea-ture. Jellinek frequently refers to the fact that the purpose of law is determined by the interests of the community (*Gemeininter-esse*)[52] and he sees this as a check upon arbitrary individual will, as a check upon both individuals and the state. "Jedes Individual-interesse," he writes, "findet rechtliche Anerkennung nur dann, wenn diese Anerkennung auch im Gemeininteresse geboten ist . . . Uberwiegend im Gemeininteresse anerkanntes individualles Inter-esse ist Inhalt öffentlichen Rechtes."[53] The content of public law is determined by the interests of the community, but important as this content is, it is not, for Jellinek, the criterion of law. Obliga-tion, as viewed by the formal liberals, is not based, in the final analysis, upon the content of law but upon the compulsion be-hind it.

Law, as understood by integral liberalism, was filled with sub-stantive, ethical content. Law was emptied of all ethical content by the formal jurists. As Heller points out, law for the integral liberal had:

Seine Eigenschaft, seine Kraft als Gesetz, seine 'Unverbruchlichkeit' . . . ausschliesslich . . . weil es als autonomer Beschluss der die Gemeinschaftswerte repräsentierenden volonte generale gilt. Von irgendeiner Verwaltungsvor-schrift oder einen Rechtsspruch unterscheidet es sich keineswegs durch seine Rechtssatzeigenschaft, sondern lediglich durch seine erhohte materielle Geltungskraft.[54]

It is form alone that distinguishes law for the positivist jurist. As Laband said on one occasion: "*es gibt keinen Gedanken, welcher nicht zum Inhalt eines Gesetzes gemacht werden konnen.*"[55] It is not the recognition of the inherent justness of the content of law that makes the individual submit to it but simply the compulsion behind it.

Law is conceived as the resultant of a conflict of individual and group interests and wills. So long as there exists a community of interests, so long as conflicting groups are convinced that the maintenance of the existing political, economic, and social system is essential to the realization of their wills, the system holds together. When, however, group interests become irreconcilable within the existing framework of political institutions, when compromise no longer satisfies them, the system crumbles under the might of the strongest group.

A political order based upon the conception of law as the resultant of the conflict of group interests and wills can only survive so long as the various groups within the system are willing to abide by certain formal, procedural rules and so long as they are willing to compromise their interests. But such a system necessarily rests upon a precarious basis and is ever prone to give way to the strongest will and interest. Without a common recognition of certain objective values, transcending subjective interests, a stable social and political order is impossible. The existence of the state demands that subjective interests be subordinated to values affirmed by all, or nearly all, of the members of the particular society. Without such an affirmation there is anarchy, and anarchy manifests itself politically as tyranny.

CHAPTER V

BEYOND GOOD AND EVIL

*Die naturwissenschaftliche Erkenntnistheorie der ge-
samten heutigen Staatslehre gestattet ihr . . . nur einen
materialistischen Realitätsbegriff, sowie dessen Kor-
relat in Gestalt eines Als-Ob-Idealismus.*

—HERMANN HELLER

MATERIALISM OR PRAGMATISM

THE EMPIRICAL THEORY of knowledge, which by the end of the
nineteenth century had been accepted almost generally, permitted,
as Hermann Heller observes above, but two alternative views of
reality. Reality could be conceived either as being composed of
matter obeying mechanical principles or as a reflection of human
purpose, that is, a fiction. In either view metaphysical considerations were ignored or denied.

Materialism, as the denial of everything supernatural, "holds
. . . that what happens in the world is never the result of the agency
of independent spiritual or mental powers, but is always explica-
ble even when, owing to the lack of sufficient knowledge, it cannot
at the time be explained 'as a consequent of the composition of
natural forces.'"[1] It affirms, as Chapman Cohen says, "the belief
that the state of the world, or of any portion of it, at any given
time, is the exact consequence of the distribution and conjunction
of forces preceding that moment."[2] It affirms a mechanical determinism.

Now the effect of this point of view upon ethics is particularly
significant. Since it denies freedom of will, for one thing, it denies
that man can be held responsible for his acts. As Joad says, " . . .
if men's wills are not free, praise is as irrelevant as blame is im-
pertinent, and *tout comprendre est tout pardonner* is the beginning
and end of ethics."[3] It removes men's acts to a realm beyond good
and evil. Since materialism denies the existence of objective values
there can be no such thing as good and bad, beautiful and ugly,
except as expressions of purely subjective feeling. Materialism
denies that there are any objective, metaphysical qualities inherent
in things or acts. Ultimate and absolute values are rejected.

---

[1] For notes to chap. v, see pp. 134–136.

The alternative view of reality permitted by the dominant empirical theory of knowledge tends to make truth relative to the observer. Moreover, it tends to identify truth "with emotional satisfaction."[4] Relativistic and subjectivistic, pragmatism denies the existence, or at least the possibility, of finally discovering absolutes and ultimates. As a practical philosophy it suggests that men should act "as if" certain things were true, irrespective of whether they actually are true or not, especially if the things assumed to be true prove emotionally satisfying and "work."[5] As Joad observes: "Pragmatism subjects truth . . . to the domination of the human mind, and insists that in the long run that alone is true which it suits human beings to think true."[6]

Pragmatism, like materialism, rejects absolute values, but it goes beyond materialism by saying that individuals are justified in acting "as if" certain things are true and good. It makes truth and good, however, relative to human beings and provides no objective standard by which truth and good may be measured. It ministers, as Joad points out, "to human complacency by assuring human beings that right and wrong, beauty and ugliness, reality and unreality, are not external facts, features of the universe to which human beings must in the long run subject themselves, but are the products of human consciousness and, therefore, *amenable to human desires*."[7] By exalting human desire to the position of a final standard for making value judgments pragmatism tends to lead, in its extreme form, to complete subjectivism and irresponsibility.

It leads to a rejection of objectivity that makes it possible for a Nazi to declare:

We perceive and acknowledge no truth for the sake of truth, no science for the sake of science. . . . If objectivity is interpreted as a pretension to the absolutism of scientific perception, as the pretension for existence apart from living foundations, then such a claim will not only be repudiated as the arrogance of a superhuman being, but the whole pretension will be unmasked as self-deception, yea, even falsehood. From our national and historical perspective we can grasp after truth, and if we seek it with sincerity, it will reveal itself to us according as our character is, and will be measured by the needs of our life.[8]

Truth and falsehood, right and wrong, beauty and ugliness, become relative to individual perspective, and, with no objective standard of truth, good, and beauty, there is no way of saying that what appears as falsehood, ugliness, or brutality viewed from one standpoint is not, indeed, viewed from another, truth, beauty, and heroism. Pragmatism ends, like materialism, by placing human acts beyond absolute judgments of good and evil.

JURISPRUDENCE BIFURCATED: NEO-KANTIANISM AND NEO-HEGELIANISM

By the end of the nineteenth century, German jurists had split into two opposing schools: the Neo-Hegelians, who focused their attention upon legal content to the exclusion of all normative considerations, and the Neo-Kantians who concerned themselves with normative elements of law to the exclusion of all consideration of legal content. Although both apparently repudiate empiricism, actually their theories are colored by one of the two alternative views of reality sketched above. The Neo-Hegelians start, consciously or subconsciously, from the point of view of materialism; the Neo-Kantians from that of pragmatism; the former are enmeshed in "factualism"; the latter in an "as-if" idealism.

Positivism had led to a complete separation of fact and standard, will and norm. It was possible now only to make one or the other absolute. They could no longer be conceived as complementary, as they had been by integral liberalism.[9] The result of this separation and of the focusing of attention upon either fact or standard to the exclusion of the other was to divorce the concept of law completely from any absolute idea of justice in the form of eternal and absolute truths transcending individuals. Both schools of thought fostered irresponsibility; the Neo-Kantians, individual irresponsibility, and the Neo-Hegelians, irresponsibility on the part of the state. In the final analysis, both placed law beyond the boundaries of good and evil. Any action was lawful, according to the Neo-Kantians, if it conformed to certain formal, procedural requirements. As the criterion of law they substituted the manner of enactment for the content of the action. The Neo-Hegelians, on the other hand, rejected all normative criteria and regarded law as a social product and instrument and distinguished it by the physical coercion behind it. Law was thought of as a social instrument and not as the embodiment of an eternal idea of right. Law was conceived as existing less to protect individual rights than to promote social ends.

As democratic institutions developed and law became identified more and more with the "will of the people," or, more specifically, with the will of the parliamentary majority, the legitimacy of law was made to depend less and less upon its content and more upon the source from which it emanated. In the last analysis *Recht* is equated with might. Coercibility, rather than morality, is the thing which distinguishes law. Whether the coercion springs from a parliamentary majority or a well-organized armed party machine is immaterial when the distinguishing criterion of law is conceived as the force behind it. When the form of law alone is considered significant there can be no substantive limitation to arbitrariness; there can be no guarantee of freedom as integral liberalism conceived of it.

By separating will and norm, interest and ideal, fact and standard, and by emphasizing one of these as the criterion of law to the exclusion of the other, responsibility is made impossible, since the idea of responsibility requires both notions. A will, unrestrained by a recognition of transcendental standards, is limited only by its physical capacity and by the might of a stronger will. A norm without a will to actualize it is equally devoid of imposing responsibility for the notion of responsibility necessarily implies *willing* to do or not to do something. Order, in the final analysis, can only rest upon compulsion, upon the will of the stronger, a will which may or may not be numerically the largest.

Both the Neo-Kantians and the Neo-Hegelians, therefore, although nominally liberals, espoused a conception of freedom that resembled license more nearly than it did the conception of freedom held by integral liberals. Under Gerber, Laband, and Jellinek, integral-liberal concepts had become formalized; under the jurists who followed them at the turn of the century, integral-liberal concepts became decadent. The vocabulary of liberalism remained but its thought had been emptied of its original substance. The formalism of Laband and Jellinek was carried to its logical extreme by the Neo-Kantians in an effort to create a "pure" science of law. Regarding jurisprudence essentially as a normative science concerned with "what ought to be" rather than with "what is," they deliberately divorced law from political and social realities and by definition removed it to a "pure" realm beyond actuality. By emphasizing norms to the exclusion of the wills that must exist in actuality in order to apply them, the Neo-Kantians postulated a realm that may have had logical but certainly not actual existence. At any rate they assumed the existence of this realm apart from social reality and acted, for the purposes of constructing a "pure theory of law," "as if" it actually existed.

The "Pure" Theory of Law

The separation of law from political and social reality, begun by Laband and Jellinek, was completed by the Neo-Kantians. In an effort to establish a "pure" science of law, jurists like Rudolph Stammler and Hans Kelsen sought to find the a priori principles or assumptions which underlie all law regardless of its content. They sought to isolate, in a Platonic sense, the "idea" of law which was universal from the content of law which was variable. They adopted for this purpose the "critical" method of Kant—a method which ignores historical development or psychological motivation in favor of a deductive search for the universal and formal elements of knowledge. They sought to find the pure forms of law, the universal elements that are found in all law. They assume, of course, that the form of law is eternal and immutable and that the content of law is ever changing.

"The pure forms . . . ," according to Stammler, "are nothing but conceptual methods of ordering."[10] It is form and form alone which possesses "absolute validity" for Stammler. He writes:

The old endeavor to obtain an ideal law with limited content is entirely futile. It is not possible to conceive of a law which would really have a content limited in subject matter but which yet would hold good for all times and peoples. *Absolute* validity of conceptions can, in *legal* questions also, be attributed only to the *pure forms,* in which we arrange *legal* experience according to a fixed and uniform plan.[111]

Here is an explicit assertion that it is not the content of law which distinguishes it from non-law but the form. Belief in eternal and absolute truths transcending individuals is abandoned completely, it is only the "idea of law" which is transcendent, which possesses "absolute validity." "There are certainly," he contends, "pure forms of juristic thought which are unconditionally necessary as ordering principles *for any content of law whatsoever.*"[12] It is these formal, universal elements that are the distinguishing criteria of law.

As Emerson points out "the unity of the pure ideas of law," for Stammler, is "only the unity of procedure by which conditioned legal prescriptions are to be determined in an identical fashion, that is, the formal unity of law is for him the unity of the method of intellectual apprehension or thinking of law."[13] "It is for the idea," Stammler writes, "to unify all the conceptually determined things under an absolute harmony."[14]

Stammler explains the "notion of law" in the following manner :

By the combination of the purposes of a number of men an external regulation is implicitly imposed upon them. They are, however, subjected to this either in an *objectively* enduring way or else according to *subjective whim* from one time to another. . . . Not until we have the *objectively enduring* type of social combination do we get the 'notion of law.' Law appears thus as a necessary part of the system of pure principles for ordering consciousness. . . . The law . . . signifies *inviolable, sovereign, combining will.*[15]

Law, for him, belongs to the realm of volition. "When we formulate a legal principle," as Ginsberg interprets Stammler, "we do not assert a fact of experience but rather an end or purpose to be fulfilled. By saying that law is a species of will we do not mean that it is created by will, or that it is its product, but that it *is* will, that is, one way in which will appears."[16] Stammler sees a social will binding men together for the purpose of achieving ends common to them all. Law is an expression of this will. It is binding on the creator as well as on the subject, independent of individual consent, *"das unverletzbar selbstherrlich verbindende Wollen."*[17]

He is somewhat vague about the binding nature of law for he says :

Law presents itself as an external regulation of human conduct. By this we understand the laying down of norms which are quite independent of the person's inclination to follow them. It is immaterial whether a person obeys them because he regards them as right, submitting out of respect for the law; or whether his obedience is due to a selfish motive of some sort, fear of punishment, or hope of reward; or, finally, whether he thinks about it at all, or acts from mere habit.[18]

Having discarded the notion of a law "whose content shall be unchangeable and absolutely valid" in favor of a "universally valid formal method, by means of which the necessarily changing material of empirically conditioned legal rules may be so worked out, judged, and determined that it shall have the quality of objective justice"[19] he has placed himself in the position of discarding natural law at the outset and then letting it in again through the back door under a different name. He repeatedly speaks of "just law" and of a "community of free-willing men" as the social ideal by means of which the justness of positive law may be determined.[20]

He postulates as the "idea of justice" a harmony of wills, the bringing of "all possibilities of desire into the one harmonious realm of the will."[21] "The content of a particular aspiration," he writes, "is then *fundamentally* right if it fits harmoniously, so far as one can see, into that totality of aims."[22] That is only possible when the individual "directs his will in the sense of what is *universally valid,* guided by the idea of perfect harmony with all other will contents."[23] His "idea of rightness," however, as Emerson points out, "is purely formal, able to take up any content."[24]

He does not think that obligation is based upon the content of law but rather upon a formal and abstract "idea of justice." He avoids answering the question whether all laws must be obeyed. "This kind of question," as Ginsberg says, "as belonging to the detailed discussion of particular legal systems, is not raised by Stammler, and in general, he leaves us rather in the dark as to how he conceives actual law to be related to right law."[25] He cannot free himself entirely from conceptions of natural law and the idea of a "higher" law creeps in despite his positivism, but since his criterion of justice is purely formal it constitutes no substantive limitation.

Society, for Stammler, is not an entity nor a personality but a community of wills.[26] Within the community each individual seeks his own subjective ends and tends to treat other individuals as means. But none of these particular subjective ends can be binding simply because it exists. For an end to be binding upon all individuals within the community it must be objective; that is, it must be common to all and independent of any particular interest peculiar to one individual or group of individuals. Now Stammler concludes that "the only things which can serve as an absolutely valid standard for all possible striving is a *purely formal* method of guidance in the shape of an ideal object of thought which directs one's judgment."[27]

Hocking explains Stammler's view as follows:

Each individual must recognize (and to some extent does recognize) the fact that his own particular ends are particular, and therefore not absolutely valid; each one conceives a condition in which he would be free from the domination of such partial objects, in view of a completely legitimate and imperative object which his purified will would seek. And if the ideal condition of purity of will (*Willensreinheit*) were reached by all, then (as we all dimly recognize) the business of bringing about social solidarity would likewise be ideally simplified; for there would be no disposition to use any member as a means, beyond the point at which he is himself served by the union, so that the united willing becomes means to his ends. Such a community would be a community of free-willing men. And this ideal of "pure community" (*reine Gemeinschaft*) is the ideal which more or less blindly stands over each actual will and constitutes the element of "right" which it recognizes in the concrete agencies of social control.[28]

Commenting on this theory, Hocking continues:

Clearing this notion of Stammler's verbiage, it seems rather an empty one—so empty indeed as to be perhaps slightly perverse. For what else does it amount to than the proposition that the whole valid end of a community is the *existence* of a community; or, that communities have nothing else to work for, in their notions of right, than simply *to be communities* in the perfect sense of that term—working out in all their arrangements the principle of consent which is involved in any free union of wills?[29]

It is difficult to see how Stammler's conception of a "pure community" of will imposes any substantive limitation upon individual will.

There is no such thing as "pure" will; there is no such thing as a will without content or aim. And where there is no common affirmation of values there can be no common will. Without a community of values the will of the community becomes for all practical purposes the will of the strongest individuals within the community. It is only possible to conceive of a community will where the existence of objective values is recognized and acknowledged as a limitation upon the individual wills and desires in the community.

Stammler provides no objective limitation to individual will and interest. He denies that there are any eternal truths and values constituting a limitation. The only limitation Stammler sees is a purely formal one. The individual can recognize no moral responsibility where no objective values exist; since Stammler denies the existence of objective values he denies that the individual has any moral responsibility. He provides no substantive limitations which might restrain the community of will from acting arbitrarily. What

Stammler has done in effect is to equate right with might. As Hocking says:

Stammler's guides are simply, as he is fond of calling them, *Richtlinien* or *Blickpunkte*, for the mind of the reflective law-maker. But there is room for skepticism as to whether such *Blickpunkte* are capable of doing actual work, or whether the work that they seem to do in Stammler's hands is done by them or by some further criterion unacknowledged or undiscovered, which the condition of *Willensreinheit* (implying a lack of strict logical deduction from criterion to application) allows to enter unobserved. It might seem as though such purely formal criteria, instead of being too rigid, as Kohler complains, are so empty of content as to permit any filling.[30]

It is just this lack of content that makes it impossible to conceive of any obligation because obligation means that you ought to will some things but not others. In order to will you have to will something; in order to will rightly you have to know *what* you ought to will. No formal method can tell you this. When the criteria of obligation are emptied of all content, when any content can be filled in, there exists no moral obligation and hence, no limitation upon will except that imposed by force!

Stammler emptied the criteria of obligation of all substantive content but Kelsen went even further. His work, as Kaufmann points out, was "the most radical attempt to carry out the pure formalism of law on the Neo-Kantian basis."[31] He concerns himself solely with the form of law, and, unlike Stammler, is not interested in the will behind the law. As Emerson observes:

Not even the factual source of the content of the norm interests him. Law can be produced—*i.e.*, logically derived—from law; if the norms of law are set by the despot, the absolute monarch, the parliament, this means, from Kelsen's stand-point, that there is logically supposed a norm authorizing these persons to fix the content of law. . . . We are in fact told no more than that, given a legal norm, we can find its logical presuppositions. The original norm at which Kelsen arrives is not to be traced back to any will; it is a purely formal concept which can be filled with any content; it is only a necessary aid to thought.[32]

In an effort to establish a "pure science of law" he completely ignores all political, social, and psychological considerations, discarding them as metajuristic.

Kelsen carries to its ultimate conclusion the endeavor, started by Gerber, Laband, and Jellinek, to eliminate all metaphysical considerations from legal theory. At the same time he endeavors to

carry on the liberal tradition by making the validity of law independent of any personal authority. He endeavors to preserve the
concept of the *Rechtsstaat* but since his theory leads to the conclusion that *every* state is a *Rechtsstaat* he deprives the concept of any
meaning given it by integral liberalism.

He distinguishes legal norms from other social norms by the
coercive force behind the former, and conceives the law as a norm
prescribing certain human behavior. As he states it:

Legal norms are coercive norms. In order to bring about the desired behavior,
the norm threatens the person disobeying it with a coercive act which he deems
as evil. . . . Thus the specific structure of a legal norm is revealed as the typical
rule of law (*Rechts-Gesetz*); it connects two facts, a certain fact, as the
condition, with another fact—the coercive act—as the consequence. The
simplest example is the norm of criminal law. If some one commits larceny,
he shall be punished. It is one of the most important contentions of the Pure
Theory of Law that the whole material of positive law can be rendered in
rules of this fundamental form.[33]

The "legal order" consists of "a plurality of norms forming one
system."[34] The unity of this order is found in the fact "that all the
norms constituting this order have the same ground of validity,
i.e., they can be traced back to one and the same basic norm."[35]

What is this basic norm? He answers: it "is the one which determines in what way the norms belonging to the order are to be
created."[36] He is somewhat vague about the nature of this basic
norm, upon which concept his whole theory rests, and he never
actually says exactly what it is. He does say that it "cannot be
'created' in the same sense as the norms of the legal order whose
unity is founded upon it," that it "is not created by the organs of
the legal order, but is presupposed by legal cognition" and "is,
therefore, not a positive but a hypothetical norm."[37]

The norms of a particular legal order acquire validity for
Kelsen as they are derived from this basic norm but the question
naturally arises as to the validity of the basic norm itself. How is
this determined? Kelsen refuses to answer, dismissing the question
as irrelevant, as raising considerations that he regards as meta-
juristic. In the final analysis the validity of the basic norm is
assumed a priori. Lauterpacht, commenting on Kelsen's theory,
says:

The norm which lies at the basis of his system, although not arbitrary, is
purely relativist and hypothetical. There is in it no such absolute element

which it would necessarily contain if it were grounded in a material ethical value, for instance, in that of justice. The initial hypothesis is an act of human intelligence. It is not a dictate of a higher power. It is not a deduction from an immutable principle of justice; it is an assumed hypothesis glorying in its realistic relativism. Kelsen claims for his initial hypothesis that it transforms might into law. However, this claim is in itself morally indifferent. Frequently such transformation will prove ethically repugnant. The fundamental norm is a methodological instrument pure and simple. It certainly substantiates Kant's dictum of "the method creating its objects."[38]

The content of law, according to Kelsen's theory, is filled in by human will and there are no substantive limitations to bind the will or direct its action. The only limitation imposed is procedural and formal. Responsible freedom as understood by integral liberalism is thus destroyed. Kelsen himself acknowledges this when he says:

Any content whatsoever can be legal; there is no human behavior which could not function as the content of a legal norm. A norm becomes a legal norm only because it has been constituted in a particular fashion, born of a definite procedure and a definite rule. Law is valid only as positive law, that is, statute (constituted) law.[39]

The content may be just or unjust, good or bad; it may be supplied by a parliament or a despot, so far as the "Pure Theory of Law" is concerned procedure alone determines the validity of law.

The state is identified by Kelsen with the legal order and hence all of its acts are legal. It cannot act illegally. As stated by Kelsen:

The Pure Theory of Law views the State as a system of human behavior, an order of social compulsion. This compulsive order is not different from the legal order for the reason that within one community only one and not two compulsive orders can be valid at the same time. Every expression of the life of a State, *every act of State, is a legal act.*[40]

Since he views the state essentially as a system of norms he tends to ignore or minimize the human agencies and organs through the medium of which the will of the state is made manifest. "A human act," he contends, "is only designated an act of State by virtue of a legal norm which qualifies it as such."[41] He tends to assume that the will of the state is somehow predetermined, somehow embodied in the legal order itself. As Emerson explains Kelsen's view:

The physical or psychical acts of the State's organs are juristically irrelevant: they are only material for attribution. The will of the State is, then, only a juristically constructed attribution point. In consequence the person of the State, like all other legal personality, is merely the personification of legal norms. . . . the State, as wholly a legal construction, has no other content than that given it by law and no acts can be attributed to it which are not foreseen by law.[42]

According to Kelsen:

Wherever anyone alleges that he acts for the State, he must be able to fall back upon a legal prescription which allows this act to appear as willed by the State, and, therefore, attributable to the State. An act of a State organ not founded on a legal prescription or statute is unthinkable in the modern *Rechtsstaat*.[43]

The *Rechtsstaat* as conceived by integral liberalism is founded upon justice, the *Rechtsstaat* as conceived by Kelsen is indifferent to justice. By definition, moreover, every state, according to Kelsen's formula, is a *Rechtsstaat*, since every state is identical with a particular legal order.

Although Kelsen gives little or no attention to the will behind the law he does accept positive law as the only law. By so doing he tacitly recognizes individual will as the sole source of the content of law. Moreover, since he believes that it is the form, rather than the content, of law which makes it binding he removes any substantive limitation to individual will. By recognizing procedure alone as a limitation, by denying that the basic norm itself must have any specific content, he actually fosters individual irresponsibility.

The only thing which constitutes a limitation is a sense of obligation on the part of the individual to follow a certain procedure in enacting law. But this sense of obligation is not grounded in conscience for conscience demands the recognition of transcendent truth and Kelsen discards this notion. Since he does discard it he has real difficulty explaining *why* the individual ought to observe legal rules, *why* a certain procedure should be followed, *why* one norm should be derived from another. He has destroyed all criteria for obligation.

Without acknowledging it, he does resort in the final analysis, through the notion of a basic norm, to natural-law concepts. He assumes that obligation is self-evident, that it is "natural." But since his positivism prevents him from appealing to ethical values he does not make out a very good case for the self-evidence of obligation. He merely states that the validity of a basic norm must be assumed as self-evident and lets it go at that. He does not appeal to the substance of the basic norm as the source of obligation and fails thereby to provide an objective basis for the sense of obligation which he presupposes. Without some belief in absolute and eternal truths and values transcending individuals the objective basis for obligation is removed and obligation becomes far from self-evident.

THE EMERGENCE OF A NORMLESS FACTUALISM

If the Neo-Kantians emphasized norms to the exclusion of wills, standards to the exclusion of facts; the Neo-Hegelians emphasized wills rather than norms, and facts rather than standards. By accepting this separation, made inevitable by positivism, both succeeded in placing law beyond good and evil, for neither could succeed in deriving from norms alone or from facts alone a legitimate and workable notion of obligation. Obligation must rest upon conscience, that is, upon a common recognition of truth and value transcending individuals, or there is no obligation in a moral sense. By denying the existence of transcendental norms filled with substantive content, both schools were forced to distinguish law by the coercion behind it. Force alone could bring law into existence, or, at least, could guarantee its existence.

One of the founders of the Neo-Hegelian school of jurists was Adolf Lasson. He espouses freedom under the law, and in this lies his claim to being a liberal, but his conceptions of freedom and of law are very different from those held by integral liberalism. Whereas Neo-Kantianism endeavored to "purify" the science of law from all social, political, and psychological elements, Neo-Hegelianism took cognizance of the fact that "the philosophy of law cannot possibly escape involving itself in the contentious social and political questions."[44]

Lasson identifies law with the will of the state. He says that the state is a *Rechtsstaat* but means by this simply "that whatever the States does it necessarily does in the form of law."[45] Like Kelsen he is driven to the conclusion that every state is a *Rechtsstaat*. As he wrote:

The State can will nothing other than the law, *i.e.*, than its own will. *Any desired content which the State wills* becomes immediately, because the State wills it, *a legal command,* and the State can will nothing other than in the form of a legal command.[46]

This sounds very much like Kelsen when he says that "every act of State is a legal act." In fact, Kelsen and Lasson reach similar conclusions though for different reasons.

Kelsen reached this conclusion because he conceived of the state as identical with the legal order, as the personification of the unity of a legal system. Lasson reached this conclusion because he conceived of the state as the supreme power within society, as the final arbiter between conflicting norms. Law for Lasson consists of all rules which are effective within society. The state, as the sole agency capable of coercing individuals because of its superior force, finally declares what is law by enforcing obedience to certain rules in the event of conflict between them.

Freedom for Lasson means freedom from all compulsion that is not legal. But, since he exalts the state to the role of supreme arbiter and contends that all action on the part of the state is legal, his conception of freedom is quite different from that held by integral liberalism. Freedom might actually become slavery. The individual, moreover, counts for little, his interests may be sacrificed to those of the state whenever the latter wills it so. For Lasson declares:

The State is the highest and last of all natural things, as the law which is the content of its will is the highest and last of all natural systems. The empirical individual is for the activity of the State nothing but an object serving the State's ends. . . . the natural individual with his interests is sacrificed for the State as soon as it is necessary.[47]

There are no human rights that set limits to the will of the state.

A somewhat less extreme position, but one which is similar, is taken by Josef Kohler. He conceives of law as being relative to particular cultures, as being at the same time a product and instrument of a culture. He rebels against the static formulas of the Neo-Kantians and emphasizes the changing needs of a dynamic society. He conceives of culture (*Kultur*) as "the greatest possible development of human knowledge and the greatest possible development of human control over nature."[48] Law can only be understood as part of a cultural pattern. For that reason he said:

Law must be different in every different Culture, in order to realize its own object. . . . There can be, therefore, no such thing as an eternal law, nor is it admissible to prophesy what shape law will take hundreds of years hence.[49]

Law is relative to time and place but all law, at all times and in all places, strives to attain one goal, namely, the "greatest possible development of human control over nature." The content of law continually changes but the goal remains the same. Kohler contends that this goal may not be achieved by the activities of individuals alone and that the final agency to carry out the cultural ends of a particular time and place is the state. The essential purpose of the state is to promote culture and if force is necessary to do so then force is justified. The promotion of culture demands the initiative of political rulers conscious of the destiny of the nation.[50]

The distinctive thing about law is the coercion behind it. "Law," Kohler writes, "is the standard of conduct which, in consequence of the inner impulse which urges men toward a reasonable form of life, emanates from the whole, and is forced upon the individual. It is distinguished from morals, customs, and religion as soon as the point is reached at which compulsory standards are separated from those demands that involve merely social amenity."[51] The individual is subordinate to the culture, and, if necessary, must sacrifice his rights and interests in favor of the requirements of the cultural community in which he lives. "The demands of culture," he writes, "often require the downfall of existing rights."[52]

This view is completely at variance with that held by integral liberalism. For liberalism the rights of individuals, as moral entities, are absolute and eternal. The state exists to preserve them. Though Kohler speaks of the state as a *Rechtsstaat,* he thinks that the state may destroy individual rights whenever it deems it necessary. He clings to the vocabulary of liberalism but gives the liberal concepts meaning which integral liberalism would repudiate.

Liberalism, in its integral form, placed the individual at the center of its thought—the preservation of the dignity of human personality was the essential function of the state and of society. Kohler bows down before inevitable "progress," a progress which may require the annihilation of human dignity and rights. For, as he observes:

It must be taken into consideration (in the errors of trial by divine judgment) that the sacrifice of the individual secured the peace of society. . . . Universal history often requires the individual to be thus sacrificed: the iron tread of progress tramples thousands underfoot. This is a terrible phenomenon which we must moderate and ameliorate as far as possible. . . . But here we must simply accept the ways of Divine Providence, in the consciousness that thus the progress of the world is accomplished.[53]

Ideas of right change with different cultures and at different times. The most one can do, according to Kohler, is to discover the ideal of a particular cultural epoch and from this forecast the immediate, but not too far distant, future. This ideal must guide the legislator and judge. More one cannot do. If one attempts to set up some absolute and eternal standard, such as human rights, one views things in a false perspective and ignores the fact that ideas of right change with changing cultural conditions.

Nothing can be declared to be eternally and absolutely right or wrong. Human rights are as relative to time and place as other things. Kohler writes:

No one who looks at the matter entirely from the standpoint of . . . human rights will be able to appreciate slavery in its historical development. Human rights are not advantageous to every development: technical arts must advance, humanity must make progress in industrial life, and for centuries this goes on with the sacrifice of human life. The sacrifice to culture is the highest sacrifice that the individual can make; but it is also one that he must make.[54]

The standard which Kohler would supply is vague for practical purposes. He admits this himself when he says:

The culture of an age is connected with the soul and spirit of a people. To fathom them is the task of folk-psychology, which it must be admitted, still needs to be greatly developed. . . . Moods follow one another owing to psychic necessity, and owing to laws that are yet partly unknown.[55]

As Hocking says, "one must be something of a seer to catch the pulse of Culture"[56] and, perhaps, only a Hitler, impressed with his own messianic mission, can actually feel the pulse of a national culture. For the ordinary legislator or judge, unimpressed with his powers as a prophet, the standard supplied by Kohler would prove impracticable as a guide. As Hocking aptly puts it, "the relation of the law-maker to Culture remains . . . that of a mystic to his deity," and, in the final analysis, "Kohler then, as well as Stammler, falls back upon intuitive judgment and upon the intuitive judgment of specially qualified minds."[57] Just as Stammler's theory fostered irresponsibility on the part of the individual, so Kohler's theory fosters irresponsibility on the part of the state.

Kohler was somewhat more temperate than other Neo-Hegelians but he did identify law with the command of the state and deny all normative limitation upon will. Other Neo-Hegelians, notably Lasson, Berolzheimer, Kaufmann, and Carl Schmitt, tended to substitute power for culture. Since Kohler himself thought of culture as control, or power, over nature, it was but a short step to substitute power for culture.

Lasson's views have been briefly mentioned above. In Berolzheimer the tendency to identify power and culture (*Kraft* and *Kultur*) is clearly manifested. He agrees with Kohler in thinking that the end of culture is to provide men with greater power over nature. This power, as it grows, is conserved by the state and is, indeed, made possible only by the existence of the state. As Emerson says, this view led him to the conclusion "that the source of objective law is 'always a factual condition of power-rulership or some other manifestation of power.'"[58] Conscious of class conflict within the modern state, Berolzheimer thought of law as having its content determined by class interests, he thought of it as the resultant of economic forces, in the final analysis as the resultant and embodiment of might.[59]

For Kaufmann, too, the state was the embodiment of power, the agency responsible for carrying out the cultural aims of a particular time and place. The state, he says, is "the organization which a people gives itself, in order to thread itself into world history and to assert its peculiar genius in it."[60] Indeed, as he put it more explicitly, "the essence of the State is the development of power, is the will to assert itself and make itself effective in world history."[61] The ideal towards which all human striving is directed is not a community of free men, as integral liberalism believed, but the victorious war.[62] For, Kaufmann believed, it is in war that a people expresses its peculiar genius at its best. The people who have the best *Kultur*, who have the greatest power, will win, and, as a consequence, war is the ultimate standard of "right." This simply means that he believes that might makes right.

The degeneracy of his "liberalism," made manifest in his writings long before 1933, was confirmed at the advent of Hitler's regime. Though himself a Jew he saluted the advent of the Nazis by saying that he had the deepest confidence in Adolf Hitler and the ethical content of his movement. Though before 1933 he had called himself a liberal, and actually fought for liberal reforms, he could say this with sincere conviction. As the brief description of his ideas shows, though a "liberal" in name, his ideas were more congenial to National Socialism than to integral liberalism. His case is typical of many "liberals" of the era just following World War I, and it illustrates the degeneracy to which liberalism had sunk in pre-Nazi Germany. It was possible for these liberals to accept Hitler, and even to acclaim him, because their concepts were congenial to National Socialism.

THE "PURE" THEORY OF POWER

Similarly, Carl Schmitt, who for a time was the "Crown jurist" of Nazism, expounded long before 1933 ideas that displayed more kinship with National Socialism than they did with integral liberalism. In *Der Begriff des Politischen,* published in 1927 when the Weimar Republic was at its height, he espoused the view that the end of all political activity is the acquisition of power for its own sake.[63] The essential function of the state is to differentiate between friend and enemy. By enemy he means simply a group struggling for its existence and opposed to another such group.

As Kolnai describes Schmitt's views:

Politics as a struggle between rival centers of power is more vital for the State than its administrative tasks and functions . . . enmity . . . is the distinctive feature of political existence—of any existence worthy of its name. . . . Just as the spheres of morality, aesthetics and utility circle around the polarities of Good and Evil, Beautiful and Ugly, Useful and Detrimental respectively—so the sphere of politics has as its characteristic the contrast between "Friend and Foe." . . . Political conflicts . . . are neither collisions of interests nor antagonisms of a "spiritual" (religious, moral, etc.) order. Since they have no bearing either on material claims or on "normative" issues of right and wrong, they *cannot be relevantly settled either by barter or by discussion and persuasion.* Their natural solution is provided by *war.*[64]

When Schmitt discusses the nature of constitutions he gives expression to this view again. The constitution of a state, he says, is not a legal norm but a conscious *existentielle* decision of the constituting power which determines the form and type of political unity desired.[65] It is immaterial what form this political unity takes or what motive prompts the decision. Whoever is capable of making this decision, moreover, is the constituting power. A constitution, Schmitt declares, does not give rise to itself but is willed into existence, and it is the force behind the will, not its normative rightness, that gives the constitution validity. As Schmitt puts it:

"Every existing political unity has its value and its authorization (*Existenzberechtigung*) not in its rightness nor in the efficacy of its norms but simply in the fact that it exists."[66] This leads him to say finally that "das Beste in der Welt ist ein Befehl."[67] The state, as the possessor of the greatest coercive power in society, as the agency capable of giving the final command, becomes completely irresponsible, ready to turn the control of its organs over to the group with the greatest power for ends which it selects.

IRRESPONSIBILITY

Thus, both Neo-Kantianism and Neo-Hegelianism led to irresponsibility—the one, to irresponsibility on the part of the individual; the other, to irresponsibility on the part of the state. One placed procedural restrictions upon individual will but left it otherwise free to do what it liked; the other subordinated individual will to the state and left the state free to pursue power for its own sake with no restriction upon the manner of acquiring power or the purpose to which this power might be put. One conceived of law as an empty form ready to be filled in with any desired content; the other conceived of law as the product and embodiment of power. Both, in somewhat different fashion, identified the state with the legal order and saw the coercive power behind the law as its distinguishing characteristic. Although some of the jurists endeavored to retain some connection between law and right, the identification remained one of vocabulary only, for they tended, in the final analysis, to identify right either with abstract formulas emptied of all content or with might.

As has been shown earlier, integral liberalism was conscious of the absolute value of human personality; above all it was imbued with the belief that each individual possesses a moral worth equal to that of every other individual. Such a belief is discarded by the jurists just considered. The Neo-Kantians are interested solely in the formal equality of individuals; the Neo-Hegelians are ready to sacrifice the individual, reluctantly in the case of Kohler, willingly in the case of Schmitt, in the interest of power.

For neither school does the individual possess inviolable rights as a human being; for neither is there a sphere of individual liberty which cannot be taken away. The Neo-Kantians would demand only that such deprivation of individual liberty be undertaken in accordance with a prescribed procedure (*any* prescribed procedure); the Neo-Hegelians would demand only that it be done for purposes of acquiring greater power for the state.

Integral liberalism espouses freedom and equality for the individual under a law that is filled with substantive and unchanging content. For both the Neo-Kantians and the Neo-Hegelians equality before the law means simply that law, whatever its content, be *applied* alike to every individual. A *Rechtsstaat* for them is not a state founded upon justice to all and each, as conceived by integral liberalism, but simply a state that issues its commands in legal form. Both schools of jurists reject the notion that there are transcendental standards filled with substantive content which bind the will of individuals and of the state. Liberal concepts, like that of the *Rechtsstaat* and of freedom, are distorted by both schools and given a meaning diametrically opposed to that ascribed to them by integral liberalism. They pay lip service to liberalism but rob it of all the meaning it originally had. Their "liberalism" is more congenial to despotism than to freedom.

CHAPTER VI

FROM NIHILISM TO TYRANNY

*Ohne politische Wertgemeinschaft gibt es weder eine
politische Willensgemeinschaft noch Rechtsgemein-
schaft. In der Auflösung dieser Wertgemeinschaft
liegen die tiefsten Wurzeln der politischen Krise
Europas.*

—HERMANN HELLER

LIBERALISM WITHOUT SUBSTANCE

HOW WAS IT POSSIBLE for prominent intellectuals, jurists, lawyers, professors, and civil servants, who before 1933 were professed liberals, to accept, and many of them to acclaim, a despotism that repudiates in word and deed the fundamental postulates of liberalism? It was possible because the "liberalism" they espoused was more closely akin to the nihilistic despotism of the National Socialists than to the doctrine whose concepts they repeated but whose substance they repudiated. They were compelled by their own logic to accept the tyranny that was forged in the crucible of intellectual and political anarchy. They had passed beyond the realm of good and evil into a realm of meaningless existence. Reason itself, as a consequence, was denied the function either of understanding the world or of ordering it. Tyranny alone could restore a semblance of order and meaning.

And these professed liberals had neither the standards nor the will to declare this despotism wrong. They could accept it only as a fact—a positive fact. The will to resist was lost—destroyed by themselves. There was, as a matter of fact, no armed resistance, no great liberal uprising against the Nazis, because the "liberals" saw nothing to fight about. They had no ideas, no values, for which to fight; they had no doctrine, no way of life, to defend.

Having denied conscience a valid role in the scheme of things, having denied the possibility of submitting opinions to a forum of reason and conscience, these professed liberals had no alternative but to accept the arena of force as the final arbiter of "right" and "justice." Having placed the law beyond good and evil, German "liberal" jurists lost by that act the capacity for condemnation. The appeal could only be made, as they themselves had taught, to

[108]

superior force. The degeneracy of liberalism was made manifest in this loss of faith in the existence of objective truth and value.

Without that faith, liberalism was but an empty husk—an empty façade. The forms of liberalism could easily be perverted, as they were, to purposes destructive of everything liberalism originally valued. Liberalism was not destroyed by the Nazis—rather, the Nazis were legitimate heirs of a system that committed suicide. Had liberalism not destroyed itself, the Nazis could never have come to power. The framework of liberalism, without the spirit of liberalism, was an ideal framework for the institution of National Socialism. A brief recapitulation may serve to clarify this thesis.

HOW LIBERALISM WAS ORIGINALLY CONCEIVED

Merged by the force of historical accident into one doctrine there are latent in liberalism as originally conceived two self-sufficient and logically independent theoretical systems.[1] When integrally conceived, liberalism postulates as its fundamental premise the absolute value of human personality. Conceiving as the essence of human individuality a God-given soul it espouses individual equality, in a spiritual sense. Each individual is regarded as potentially worthy of salvation, in the sense of fulfilling his destiny or function in the light of his talents and capacity. Hence, individuals are never means but always, as equal moral entities, ends in themselves.

Accordingly, liberalism champions individual autonomy, that is, freedom from all arbitrary compulsion, since compulsion is incompatible with the conception of human dignity. For only by the freeing of the individual from arbitrary restraints can he develop his talents and express his personality in the realization of all his potentialities. The individual is not conceived as being free to do anything he pleases or desires; he is free only to follow the dictates of reason and conscience.

As its ideal, therefore, liberalism posits freedom under the impersonal rule of law, the law being conceived as filled with certain eternal, objective truths and values discoverable by reason. The existence of objective truth and value, of transcendental standards, is presupposed (the seventeenth-century Christian mind could not do otherwise).

---

[1] For notes to chap. vi, see pp. 136–138.

Liberalism, on the other hand, conceived of society as being composed of atomic, autonomous individuals with wills and interests peculiar to themselves. (This view was fostered by the rediscovery of man's ego by the Renaissance and by the concepts of modern science.) There is ascribed to the individual the capacity to will freely. But how is it certain that the individual will not will that which is personally desirable rather than that which is objectively demanded? There is no certainty. Only a conscientious sense of duty bids the individual to follow the dictates of reason rather than those of personal interest. *For liberalism acknowledges no limitation upon individual will except that imposed by conscience.* Order, then, is potentially embodied in the existence of objective truth discoverable by reason; but, in the final analysis, it is conscience *alone* that bids the individual to reason objectively, to discover the content of true law, to translate potential order into actuality. Conscience, however, is not a subjective feeling of preference, not an instinctive intuition, but rather is a common knowledge, or recognition, of values transcending individuals. The true law, accordingly, to which individuals owe obedience, the law under which freedom is assured, is that law whose content is found in human conscience. It is in obedience to that law that the individual finds his real freedom and secures the dignity of his existence as a human being.

Two Theories of Law in Liberalism

Two logically independent notions of law, then, are latent in liberalism. First of all, there is the notion that law is the product of individual wills, of consent, and the expression of subjective interests. On the other hand, there is the notion that law is the embodiment of certain objective truths and values, in a sense found and not made. In the first view, it is the irrational compulsion behind the law which makes the individual submit to it; in the second view, it is the rational recognition of objective truth that imposes obligation. The legal order is justified, in the first instance, because it is the collective expression of individual wills and interests; it is justified, in the second instance, because of the inherent justness of the content which it embodies, independent of individual will or interest. The validity of law, in the one concept, rests upon the force behind it; in the other, upon the recognition of the inherent rightness of the content of law. The source of law is thought of, in the one concept, as individual wills; in the other, as reason, nature, or the "order of things." The validity of law, in the first instance, rests simply on the fact that the competent authority, possessed of superior coercive power, has prescribed it. In the second case the validity of law rests upon its content, upon its inherent rightness or justice. The bases of validity, therefore, are, in the one case, *formal*, and, in the other case, *substantive*.

Since the freedom that liberalism espouses is freedom under the law, the conception of law that liberals accept has significant implications for the development of liberalism. Now so long as, and to the extent that, liberals retained the substantive, as well as the formal, conception of law (that is, so long as liberals believed that law should embody certain substantive truths and values transcending individual will and interest), liberalism retained its integral character. When, however, the formal conception of law alone was retained, liberalism became decadent, preparing the way for its own demise. For the sloughing off of objective values and truths left only the subjective and anarchical elements of liberal thought; will was left without any substantial limitation. The way was now prepared for the arbitrary subjection of one individual to the will of another which meant the destruction of the dignity and freedom of human personality.

THE DECLINE OF LIBERALISM IN GERMAN THOUGHT

In Germany the formal idea of law rose to an ascendant position in the latter part of the nineteenth century, finding notable expression in the writings of jurists like Gerber, Laband, and Jellinek. Their formalism was carried to its logical extreme at the turn of the century by the Neo-Kantians, and particularly by Kelsen. But if the Neo-Kantians emphasized norms to the exclusion of wills, the Neo-Hegelians emphasized wills to the exclusion of norms, contenting themselves with a normless "factualism." And since no valid obligation can be deduced from either the realm of *Sollen*, or the realm of *Sein*, when each is focused separately to the exclusion of the other, the Neo-Kantians actually fostered irresponsibility on the part of the individual and the Neo-Hegelians irresponsibility on the part of the state conceived as a real person. Both schools of thought represent liberalism in decadence.[2]

Of the factors which contributed to the decline of liberalism in German politico-legal thought, the most important was the gradual infiltration of positivism into all realms of thought and the consequent rise to ascendancy of the subjective elements of liberal thought over the objective elements. If it is possible to formulate any "law" of development peculiar to liberalism, at least as it applies to German politico-legal thought, then that "law" is that the decline of liberalism parallels the degree to which liberal thinkers have accepted positivism—an acceptance, moreover, that appears, in retrospect at least, to have been inevitable.

Positivism, as a perspective growing out of science, denies, at least in its extreme form, the existence of values as scientifically relevant facts. In an endeavor to observe and describe "pure" facts, that is, things experienced by ordinary sense perception, positivism tends to regard all value judgments as expressions simply of subjective individual preference or feeling. The positivist denies the existence of objective values because he feels that he cannot empirically demonstrate their existence. He believes that it is possible to observe and describe facts of experience, without recourse to value judgments, and contents himself with the "pure" description of these "facts." Relying heavily upon quantitative methods of thinking, and upon "exact" measurement, his inability to measure values quantitatively lends, he believes, further validity to his argument for rejecting them as facts.

Now during the nineteenth century, particularly in Germany, science, by stimulating inventions and improving the methods of production, added greatly to the material prosperity, comfort, and security of large numbers of people. To many the practical applications of scientific discovery seemed to herald the dawn of millennium. The nineteenth century was, as Ortega y Gasset points out, an age of plenitude and self-satisfaction.[3] Where formerly, as Tillich says, men looked to God and religion for salvation they now looked to technicism and science.[4] The promise of an earthy utopia was substituted for the promise of eternal spiritual salvation as an aspiration worthy of men's efforts. The method had been found; paradise on earth waited only upon the proper execution of the plan to be discovered in the truths and methods of science. Science had become enthroned as the final arbiter of truth and value, occupying a position similar to that of the Church in the Middle

Ages. Men now turned to science for understanding and salvation, as in the Middle Ages men turned to theology and to the Church. Technical efficiency and mechanical certainty became the ideals of the nineteenth century. They were the ideals not only of the scientist but also of the dominant, satiated, bourgeoisie whose primary desires, unlike those of their seventeenth-century progenitors, were for certainty, security, and stability.

By the end of the nineteenth century, and especially in Germany, science had achieved a prestige never accorded it before. Few, if any, could resist the dominant intellectual current of the age. And it is not strange, but rather, on the contrary, inevitable that students of social phenomena should have turned with eagerness to the methods that seemed to yield predictability, certainty, and security. Hoping to achieve for the study of human phenomena the same calculable certainty that seemed to characterize the natural sciences, students of social phenomena accepted the perspective of positivism and empiricism. It is inconceivable that they should have failed to do so.

Now when integral-liberal concepts are examined in this perspective they undergo radical changes in meaning. The potential, rational order of integral liberalism filled with truths and values transcending individuals is replaced by the conception of an immanent order obeying mechanical principles. This conception of a "natural" order is more congenial to the nineteenth-century mind, moreover, since it ministers to the complacent belief in mechanically inevitable progress. It requires, indeed, no actualization by individual wills since it is an immanent order already realized and in operation. Individual responsibility tends to disappear and, in any case, is assigned a minor role. It is no longer a question of choosing the right way but of obeying that which is compelled.

When law is viewed from the standpoint of positivism, "true" law appears to be not that which is secured transcendentally but rather, simply and purely, a product of the strongest will within the community, whether the will be that of the numerical majority or the numerical minority. Positive law appears to be the only "real" law since it is the only law that can be empirically experienced. It cannot be a product of reason but only a product of will. It cannot embody truths and values transcending individuals but only desires and interests peculiar to particular individuals living at a certain time in a certain place. The task of the jurist is no longer a creative but simply an analytical one. The reason individuals submit to law cannot be the inherent justice of the law (since justice is a metaphysical concept) but simply the compulsion behind the law. By logical implication, if not explicitly, the formal liberal jurists of the late nineteenth century came close to saying that law is the command of superior force.[5] And by so saying they anticipated the brutal nihilism of National Socialism.

When the rights of man were focused with the perspective of positivism they no longer appeared as natural rights but as legal rights. When the formal liberal jurist spoke of individual rights he meant something quite different from the integral liberal. For man he substituted citizen, for the individual as a total personality engaged in manifold activities he substituted the individual as a political unit. By this device it was possible to talk of political freedom and political equality without considering the problem of economic freedom and economic equality. For substantive truths was substituted formal procedures. And by that very device the freedom and equality championed by the formal liberals became a formal freedom and a formal equality.

With the infiltration of positivism into German politico-legal thought the idea of a *Rechtsstaat* as a state limited by considerations of justice and rights peculiar to individuals by virtue of their humanity degenerates into the notion of a state limited by formal procedures. As Hermann Heller says, "A *Rechtsstaat* now is every state in which the action of the government is limited by some laws. . . . Freedom means bourgeois-economic security from such state intervention in the freedom and property of citizens to which the representatives of the people have not consented. Equality is no longer concrete opposition to injustice and arbitrariness, *i.e.*, qualitative justice, but quantitative logical universality. *Recht aber immer und alles, was die Staatsgewalt von sich gibt.*"[6] Equality before the law comes to mean equal application of the law irrespective of the just or unjust content of the law. But such a conception is obviously quite different from the integral liberal concept that envisioned, as its ideal at least, the securing equally to each man his rights. For the integral liberal there existed a sphere of individual rights into which the state might not penetrate and for the preservation of which the state existed. The dividing line between individual and state activity was fixed sharply by substantive limitations to state activity. These substantive limitations disappear in the writings of the formal liberals and are replaced by purely formal limitations—which, in effect, are no limitations at all.

OBJECTIVE IDEALITY VS. SUBJECTIVE REALITY

The full effect of positivistic thinking is seen in the twentieth century though anticipated in the latter half of the nineteenth. In twentieth-century German jurisprudence it is made manifest in the complete separation of fact and standard and in the emphasis of one of these to the exclusion of the other. But, since a principle of obligation cannot be derived from either considered alone, both schools of thought foster a complete irresponsibility that leads to anarchy. An emphasis upon normative standards that ignores social realities leads to empty abstractions, while an emphasis upon social facts to the exclusion of all normative considerations leads to an equally meaningless perspective. And this emptying of all meaning by the positivists extended, as Hermann Heller points out, not alone to the sphere of jurisprudence but to all culture—"all life appeared as a functionless and valueless sociological problem."[7]

The effects of the positivistic perspective are as evident in the realms of economics, religion, and art as they are in jurisprudence. The separation of fact from standard in jurisprudence was not an isolated phenomenon but rather part of a general phenomenon that was profound and far-reaching. The twentieth-century tendency to separate rigidly the realm of "what is" from the realm of "what ought to be" that has already been described in jurisprudence is found in other realms as well.

Kelsen's efforts to create a "pure" theory of law find parallel efforts among certain economists to create a "pure" science of economics. In their attempts to reduce the study of economics to mathematical formulas divorced from all institutional considerations we find the same effort to create a normative science of "what ought to be" divorced from all considerations of any particular social reality. On the other hand, just as Kelsen's extreme formalism is countered by the rebellion of the Neo-Hegelians so the institutional economists have challenged with their normless factualism the abstractions of the mathematical economists. By denying the existence of normative standards the institutional economists must content themselves with indifferent description having lost the capacity and method for evaluation. On the other hand, the mathematical economists escape to a world of formulas that bears little or no resemblance to the world of economic reality. Both schools of thought, albeit for different reasons, foster irresponsibility. Neither has the ability to say which course of action, in the real world, is better.

In the field of painting similar phenomena are made most manifest in Expressionism, on the one hand, and Cubism, on the other. The tumultuous emotionalism of Expressionism sought to depict the "real facts" of life in their naked "reality" with no regard for formal principles of expression. Form was deliberately distorted as color became the essential element of a painting. Just as the Neo-Hegelian jurists refused to be bound by normative considerations so the Expressionists rejected formal principles of artistic expression as outmoded encumbrances. Subjectivism run wild is characteristic of both, and unrestrained emotionalism bordering on the psychotic presages in both the beginning of an era of nihilism. For the Cubists, on the other hand, subject matter was unimportant. It was not *what* one painted, but *how* one painted that mattered, just as in Neo-Kantian jurisprudence it was not what was enacted that was significant but how the law came into being. For both, formal procedures were more important than factual content. Picasso's belief that "pure" form could be described in geometric terms is shared by the Neo-Kantians and the mathematical economists. And, like these two, Cubism is of necessity highly abstract, intellectual, analytical, and unemotional. If Expressionism robbed life, as it experienced it, of all objective meaning, then Cubism fostered a conception of life as an empty abstraction. Both succeeded in creating an art that, in the final analysis, was nihilistic.

In music these extreme positions are represented by Schoenberg and Stravinsky. In the atonal music of the former all "meaning" is obliterated in an attempt to compose entirely in terms of formal, mathematical principles. The purely cerebral, unemotional, and rigid character of his music suggests a kinship to the formalism of the Neo-Kantians, the mathematical economists, and the Cubists. On the other hand, the combination of tonalities at one time, the absence of a regular rhythm, the deliberate attempt to avoid formal arrangement that characterize the music of Stravinsky suggest a kinship to the same perspective that produced the Neo-Hegelians in jurisprudence and the Expressionists in the realm of painting.

The infiltration of positivism into the sphere of religion had the effect of forcing liberal theologians into the extreme positions of either world-affirmation, or world-denial, into the position of linking inseparably the gospel of salvation with science and industrialism or of retreating to an abstract, religious formalism.[8] One sought to find salvation by serving man rather than by worshipping God, whereas the other sought to find salvation by ignoring man and worshipping God in a purely formal way. The attitude of world-affirmation is best represented by the so-called Humanists, while the attitude of world-denial finds its best expression in the writings of Karl Barth. One attitude, by the optimistic identification of evil with ignorance, removes all transcendental barriers to the exercise of individual will, while the other, by regarding man as an essentially sinful creature incapable of improving the world as it is, leaves the individual in the real world with no practical standards or hope for exercising his will in a good and constructive way. Horton summarizes the difficulty well when he says:

Barthianism seems as wide of the mark on one side as humanism is on the other; it is an unstable combination of a crude realism with respect to man and a wistful idealism with respect to ultimate reality, just as humanism is an unstable combination of a crude realism with respect to ultimate reality and a wistful idealism with respect to man.[9]

The separation of form from content, standards from facts, principles from "reality," and the concomitant endeavor to emphasize one aspect of reality to the exclusion of the other, in an effort either to formulate a "pure" theory of existence or to achieve a "real" description of "life as it actually is," is a general phenomenon peculiar to the Western world at the end of the nineteenth and beginning of the twentieth centuries. This phenomenon finds expression in jurisprudence but it is not peculiar to jurists alone. Rather it is a manifestation of an intellectual climate and perspective found in all fields of study, in all walks of life, and in all attempts to describe "reality." Whether "reality" is thought to consist of a normless factualism or of abstractions, life tends to be robbed of all meaning. Both lead to nihilism.

But if the liberal ideology is emptied of all substantive meaning by the infiltration of positivism into all realms of thought, the liberal way of life is undermined by the gradual disappearance of individual autonomy and initiative in social and economic life. Social and economic conditions that emphasize the undesirability, if not the impossibility, of individual autonomy and initiative challenge in fact the individual freedom that positivism challenges in theory.

Problems that were once in fact individual problems amenable to individual solutions became in the nineteenth century social problems requiring social solutions. More and more individuals turned, of necessity, to organization in an effort to do collectively what they were once able to do alone. And more and more activities required more complex social organization for their successful accomplishment. And as conditions proved less and less amenable to individual efforts, the ideal of individual effort itself appeared necessarily impracticable. The ideal of individual liberty appeared to be either illusory or meaningless. As Niemeyer aptly observes:

> In proportion as social conditions condition a type of individual incapable of autonomous and independent decisions, individuals lose the faculty of judging the value of political actions by a yardstick of non-political derivation. Political power, being the instrument of the centralmost coördination of social energies, becomes identified with his existence. He ceases to be aware of standpoints from which to measure the value of political facts, other than by their political successfulness. All this tends to eliminate the humanistic criterion of value from our system of social standards.[10]

Without the ideal of the absolute value of human personality, without an environment congenial to the exercise of individual autonomy and responsibility, liberalism had, of necessity, to disappear as a dominant and effective ideology.

THE MEANING OF NAZIISM

The philosophy of individualism demands not only an appreciation of the subjective interests and wills of individuals but also a recognition of objective limits to those interests and wills. When the link between subjective interests and objective limitations is destroyed individualism degenerates into an irresponsible subjectivism—into anarchy. When all substantive limitation to individual will is removed, the way is prepared, and of necessity, either for anarchy or for tyranny. It was the degeneracy of liberalism that made tyranny in Germany possible, if not indeed, inevitable. It was the degeneracy of liberalism that fostered the irresponsibility, the arbitrary compulsion, against which liberals originally rebelled. Perhaps the fatal mistake of liberalism was the optimistic attempt to equate sin with ignorance. Describing contemporary liberals Lewis Mumford says:

Their color-blindness to moral values is the key to their political weaknesses. Hence they cannot distinguish between barbarism and civilization. . . . Refusing to recognize the crucial problem of evil, the pragmatic liberals are unable to cope with the intentions of evil men. They look in vain for mere intellectual mistakes. . . . Evil . . . has no positive dimensions.[10]

And Aurel Kolnai observes:

In its cult of "relativism," "tolerance," and "indifferentism," in its explanation of social phenomena by "psychology," or by a succession of different "modes of general outlook" or world attitudes of mind, the Liberal Spirit has definitely over-reached itself.

Here is a mood of meek generosity and arbitrary irresponsibility, which throws the door wide open to the wildest subjectivism on the one hand and arbitrary despotism on the other; subjectivism in those who delight in the pose of comfortable inertia and aesthetic passivity; despotism in those who are unable or unwilling to accept that pose.

Mincing criticism ends in shameless irrationalism; over-refined scientific scepticism in brutal pragmatism; distrust of the mind, in a return to fetishistic tribalism; "breadth of mind" in the cowardly acceptance of tyranny and class or national exclusiveness.[11]

Lacking the capacity to make value judgments the degenerate liberal has no means of protecting the individual rights which integral liberals fought with conviction to establish. Liberalism destroyed its own convictions by denying validity to conscience in its attempt to be scientific. Without a common knowledge of objective truths and values, liberalism cannot help but degenerate into anarchy. And anarchy manifests itself politically in tyranny.

The political success of the National Socialist movement in Germany can best be understood as a corollary of the failure of liberalism to retain its substantive content. The political success of the movement is best characterized, as has been done by Hermann Rauschning, as "the revolution of nihilism."[12]

So long as men find some correlation between the ideals of the dominant ideology of a period and the institutions that are established to translate these ideals into actuality the order which results appears rational, understandable, secure, and healthy. When, however, the institutions no longer appear to fulfill the promises for which they were created the order dissolves into anarchy, the system appears irrational, breeding insecurity and discontent.

Liberal political and economic institutions held out to men the promise of freedom and equality. When, in the nineteenth century, freedom degenerated into license, when substantive equality of opportunity degenerated into formal equality before the law, men began to lose their faith in liberal political institutions. Even the values upon which the liberal order were based seemed to many illusory, if not, indeed, nonexistent.

Believing against belief, the German people turned to men who promised to bring order out of chaos, to men who promised them some sense of security, to men whose program consisted of negative criticisms of a system already in ruins. If the Nazis gave the German people nothing which they could positively affirm at least they provided criticisms of a degenerate liberal system which nearly all could acclaim. It was not that the people believed in National Socialism so much as that they disbelieved in the promises of the liberal era. Fascism, as one author has ably demonstrated, came in by default.[13]

With the values of the liberal era destroyed long before Hitler ever came upon the scene the great mass of German people were prepared to will to believe in a new authority that promised by the mere act of homage to restore a feeling, at least, of certainty. As pragmatists they were prepared to act "as if" Hitler were always right. And it is upon this fiction of the infallibility of the leader, upon this "as-if idealism," that the structure of National Socialism rests. It will collapse only when the fiction itself is abandoned. To maintain that fiction is one of the essential tasks of the Propaganda Ministry and of the military organization. Only decisive military defeat can shake this fiction of infallibility—only then will the German people be able to perceive other alternatives to a tyranny they accept now as the only alternative to chaos.

Disillusioned with the promises of liberalism (and of socialism), disillusioned with the processes of reason itself, the German people have hoped, however unwisely, to create a new reality simply by emotionally affirming its existence. In their despair they have chosen to place their faith in the infallibility of Hitler; and that faith, however paradoxically, is renewed, as Peter Drucker has pointed out, from the depths of an ever increasing despair. Now they believe that they must believe in Hitler or perish. This apparent paradox is explained by Drucker in this way:

The masses must have something. . . . Though they are deeply dissatisfied with what totalitarianism has to offer, they cannot get anything else. Therefore totalitarianism must be the valid answer. The less satisfied they are with what it gives, the more must they try to persuade themselves that it is enough. . . . They are deeply unhappy, deeply disappointed, deeply disillusioned. But they must force themselves with all their power to believe in totalitarianism just because they are disillusioned and dissatisfied. . . . They are like drug addicts who have to take increasing doses of the poison, knowing it is poison, but unable to give it up because they must find oblivion and the happiness of the dream. . . .

The intellectual tension of this constant self-persuasion to believe against belief, to trust against evidence, and to cheer spontaneously after careful rehearsal is so great that no amount of self-doping could keep it from snapping. An entity must be found in which the contradiction resolves itself. Since there can be no entity within the realm of reason, it must be found in that of mysticism. . . . And since the totalitarians have no God, they must invent a Demon, a superman and magician in whom the contradictory becomes one. To be this demon in whom wrong is right, false true, illusion reality, and emptiness substance is the function of the "leader."[14]

Real consent is a spontaneous expression of approval. It is a positive force arising out of inner conviction. It is not synonymous with passive acquiescence or voluntary submission. It is found as the basis of government in greater proportion to constraint only in nations where there is a community of values and interests, that is, where there is positive affirmation of certain fundamental values and interests common to nearly all individuals and groups within the nation. It is, indeed, the existence of this community of values and interests that makes democratic, parliamentary government possible. A minority will agree to temporary rule by the majority only because certain common interests in maintaining the political system transcend partisan interests. The breakdown of democracy comes when this community of values disintegrates, when common agreement on fundamentals no longer exists, when partisans no longer endeavor to work through the state but to become the state.

The existence of real consent implies the existence of some common values and interests. It is this fact which makes it impossible for the Nazi government to secure real consent for its rule; it helps to explain why terroristic tactics, centralized propaganda control, and the extension of political supervision over all phases of life are necessary elements of Nazi rule. For it was only with the break-down of a common set of values and interests that the Nazis were able to come to power. Dictatorship, despite its ostensible appear-ance of order, is actually the government peculiar to anarchy.

Totalitarian dictatorship is the political manifestation of nihil-ism. It emerges when the belief is dominant that:

Life has no "aim." Mankind has no "aim." . . . Life is the beginning and the end . . . life has no system, no program, no reason; it exists for itself and by itself . . . it cannot be dissected according to good or bad, right or wrong, useful and desirable.[15]

That belief became dominant in Germany with the disintegration of integral liberalism, with the infiltration of positivism into every realm of thought.

The forces that produced the Nazi dictatorship in Germany were and are not peculiar to Germany alone. National Socialism, the totalitarian dictatorship, is not peculiarly a national, geographical, or temporary aberration. The same forces are at work in every other nation of the Western world. The spiritual crisis out of which totalitarianism emerged is a crisis, peculiar not to Germany, but to Western civilization.

NOTES

NOTES TO CHAPTER I

INTEGRAL LIBERALISM AND THE PROCESS OF FORMALIZATION

[1] Karl Mannheim, *Ideology and Utopia* (translated by L. Wirth and E. Shils, 1936), p. 3.

[2] Perception itself involves selection and choice. Of necessity perception demands the ordering of sensory data into some meaningful pattern. No individual is equally aware of all the possible data that may be brought to his attention by means of his sense organs. If he were, he would *perceive* nothing, his environment would appear as a chaos of sensations, unintelligible and meaningless. It is by a process of selection that perception itself is possible. The relative value attached to sensory data depends in part upon the context in which it appears and in part upon the individual's insight into the situation of the moment. (Cf. Wolfgang Köhler, *The Place of Value in a World of Facts*, 1938.)

[3] Thus, a "fact," as Professor L. J. Henderson defines it for the purposes of the scientist is "an empirically verifiable statement about phenomena in terms of a conceptual scheme" (quoted by Crane Brinton, *The Anatomy of Revolution*, 1938, p. 19). Science itself is premised upon certain metaphysical assumptions which for its purposes it must accept as true; see A. N. Whitehead, *Science and the Modern World* (1925). Science is a method of thought, "a creation of the human mind, with . . . freely invented ideas and concepts." Like every method of thought it is based upon certain presuppositions that provide a framework in terms of which "facts" may be observed and ordered. See Albert Einstein and Leopold Infeld, *The Evolution of Physics: The Growth of Ideas from Early Concepts to Relativity and Quanta* (1938).

[4] Whitehead, *op. cit.*, p. 71.

[5] Reinhold Niebuhr, *The Nature and Destiny of Man* (1941), Vol. I, p. 61.

[6] Whitehead, *op. cit.*, p. 83.

[7] Ernest Troeltsch, "The Ideas of Natural Law and Humanity in World Politics," in Otto Gierke, *Natural Law and the Theory of Society, 1500 to 1800* (translated by Ernest Barker, 1934), p. 205.

[8] Hugo Grotius, *Prolegomena*, Bk. I, ch. i, sec. xi. (Whewell's ed., 1853.)

[9] Roscoe Pound, *The Spirit of the Common Law* (1921), p. 88.

[10] *Ibid.*, p. 89.

[11] *Loc. cit.* Italics mine.

[12] Quoted by Pound, *op. cit.*, p. 90. Italics mine.

[12] For further explanation of the merging of these two theories of law see Gerhart Niemeyer, *Law Without Force: The Function of Politics in International Law* (1941), ch. iv. In part he says:

"The vain attempts, during the sixteenth century, to achieve a religious peace both of arms and of minds, resulted in a widespread abandonment of the theological approach to problems of world order, and the corresponding growth of a belief in 'scientific' methods of solving these problems. Scientific methods meant on the one hand the application of rational arguments instead of those based on revelation; on the other hand it meant that problems had to be analyzed and solved in terms of observed facts and perceivable experience. According to this shift of emphasis from mysticism to 'realism,' and from religion to science, the main object of analysis and investigation became necessarily the empirical reality of nature. In the case of legal problems this meant the focusing of attention on the empirical nature of man. . . .

"Following the discovery of the dynamics of the *Ego* during the Renaissance, and following the anthropological trends in Humanism, the idea was established that the immutable reality underlying all social and legal problems was the nature of individual man. In accordance with this 'natural' essence of every order, it was believed that inherent in human nature were certain fixed conceptions, certain laws of social structure and relationships, which called everywhere for the same basic forms of morality, legal order and economic conditions. Thus the focal point of all thinking in moral and social sciences became the individual person, typified and standardized through the conception of 'man in the state of nature.'

"If legal and political thinking begins by positing the notion of a solitary individual and then proceeds to compose society of a multitude of Robinson Crusoes, the first and basic assumption must logically be that of the natural liberty of the individual persons. . . . From the notion of originally free and independent wills of originally separate persons to the idea of legal order there leads only one logical way: that of the voluntary submission of the individual person to common authority or to common rules. The idea of contract . . . is the only possibility of making compatible the concept of 'natural' freedom with that of legal bonds" (*ibid.*, pp. 139–140).

But self-sufficient as this theory was it was not the sole source of the integral liberal's conception of law. For there lingered in the early liberal's mind the medieval conception that law is "the very essence of things, eternally underlying all relationships, independent of personal desires or wills. Law is not made, at any rate not by human wills; it is in being because the creation in itself is ordered and cannot be imagined in any other way but in orderly structure. Law is not created: it is recognized by human reason. It is inherent in the nature of created things, and has only to be found and brought to light, in which process the human will may play an auxiliary role as an agent of practical formulations applied to concrete circumstances" (*ibid.*, p. 144). These two theories of law, though logically independent, were merged by the force of historical circumstance into one conception. "The tenets of Christian faith were still too powerfully dominant to admit the conception of legal order entirely in terms of personal wills and personal interests. A legal order consisting merely in a mutual adjustment of interests on the basis of expediency would not have appeared as binding to the Christian mind of those times. Thus, torn and undecided between two eras, the seventeenth century mind had to merge the mediaeval idea of an absolute order as the essence of reality with the Renaissance conception of the individual person as the ultimately moving force in legal order. The merger . . . was not dictated by logical necessity, but by emotional forces which, though conflicting, coincided in the mentality of the seventeenth century" (*ibid.*, pp. 145–146).

[13] See Max Weber, *The Protestant Ethic and the Spirit of Capitalism* (translated by Talcott Parsons, 1930). Capitalism is something more than a mode of production. It is as much a mode of thought as it is a technological system of production. Capitalism as an economic system was as dependent upon the individualistic *Weltanschauung* that emerged with the Renaissance and Reformation as was liberalism.

[14] *Cf.* Herman Heller, *Die politischen Ideenkrise der Gegenwart* (1926), p. 19.

[15] Edmund Wilson, *Axel's Castle: A Study of the Imaginative Literature of 1870–1930* (1931), p. 3.

[16] Troeltsch, *op. cit.*, p. 210.

[17] *Loc. cit.*

[18] Troeltsch, *op. cit.*, p. 212.

[19] *Loc. cit.*

[20] Troeltsch, *op. cit.*, p. 214.

[21] Wilson, *op. cit.*, p. 6.

[22] Pound, *op. cit.*, pp. 151–152.

[23] *Ibid.*, p. 151.

[24] Fritz Ermarth, *The New Germany: National Socialist Government in Theory and Practice* (1936), p. 5.

[25] Ermarth aptly observes that "the legal state was a mechanism devised primarily to achieve and maintain the supremacy of the law. It pretended to be the human instrument of a superhuman idea of law. But the idea of law could serve as ethical justification for the existence of state power only as long as the law maintained its vital connection with the idea of justice. (Recht.) As the final and most important result of the economic development, this vital connection between the legal state and the idea of justice was destroyed. Social inequality and social injustice brought about by capitalism transformed the principle of equality that had served as an ethical basis for the legal state into a purely formalistic concept. The efforts of the legal state to provide justice among individuals were deprived of their ethical meaning through a growing social injustice. Material injustice and inequality among the social groups increased in spite of and even because of the rules that were enforced among the individuals by the state in the name of law and justice" (*op. cit.*, p. 22).

NOTES TO CHAPTER II

INTEGRAL LIBERALISM

[1] A. D. Lindsay, "Individualism," *Encyclopaedia of the Social Sciences* (hereafter cited as *E.S.S.*), (8 Vol. edition, 1937), Vol. IV.

[2] *Ibid.*

[3] *Ibid.*

[4] *Ibid.*

[5] Albert Einstein and Leopold Infeld, *The Evolution of Physics: The Growth of Ideas from Early Concepts to Relativity and Quanta* (1938), pp. 57–58.

[6] *Ibid.*, p. 58.

[7] Quoted by Einstein and Infeld, *ibid.*, p. 58.

[8] See *ibid.*, pp. 71 ff.

[9] See A. N. Whitehead, *Science and the Modern World* (1925), pp. 145 ff.

[10] W. M. Horton, *Realistic Theology* (1934), p. 117.

[11] See E. C. Moore, *An Outline of the History of Christian Thought Since Kant* (1912), ch. iii.

[12] Horton, *op. cit.*, p. 119.

[13] Adam Smith, *Wealth of Nations* (Cannan edition, 1904), Bk. IV, ch. i, p. 421.

[14] Charles Gide and Charles Rist, *A History of Economic Doctrines from the Time of the Physiocrats to the Present Day* (translated by R. Richards, 1916), p. 89.

[15] Smith, *op. cit.*, Bk. V, ch. i, part iii, art. 1.

[16] Gide and Rist, *op. cit.*, p. 96.

[17] See J. B. Say, *Le Traité d'économique politique* (1803); F. Bastiat, *Les Harmonies économiques* (1850); I. A. Schlettwein, "Theuersten Väter und Mütter der Staaten," in *Schriften für alle Staaten zur Aufklärung der Ordnung der Natur in Staatsregierungs- u. Finanzwesen* (1775); C. J. Kraus, *Staatswirtschaft* (1808); A. F. Lueder, *Ueber Nationalindustrie und Staatswirtschaft* (1800); and see particularly J. P. Köhler, "Staat und Gesellschaft in der deutschen Theorie der auswärtigen Wirtschaftspolitik und des internationalen Handels von Schlettwein bis auf Fr. List und Prince-Smith," *Beihefte zur Vierteljahrschrift für Sozial- und Wirtschaftsgeschichte,* VII (1926).

[18] Köhler, *op. cit.*, pp. 22–46.

[19] See H. Heller, *Die politischen Ideenkrise der Gegenwart* (1926), p. 81.

[20] Quoted by Heller, *ibid.*, p. 82.

[21] Cf. Köhler, *op. cit.*, p. 63.

[22] Cf. *ibid.*, pp. 50–116.

[23] *Ibid.*, p. 117.

[24] G. H. Sabine, *A History of Political Theory* (1937), pp. 432–433.

[25] Wilhelm von Humboldt, *Ideen zu einem Versuch die Grenzen der Wirksamkeit des Staates zu bestimmen* (1851), p. 15. This work was written in 1791 but published as a whole posthumously. Portions of it appeared at the time it was written in Schiller's *Thalia* and the Berlin *Monatsheft.*

[26] Kant, *Grundlegung zur Metaphysik der Sitten* (R. Otto, ed., Gotha, 1930), Sec. II.

[27] Fichte, "Grundlage des Naturrechts nach Principien der Wissenschaftslehre," *Sämmtliche Werke* (1845), Vol. III, p. 101. This work first appeared in 1796. Fichte was born in 1762 and died in 1814. As an inspired leader he did much to stimulate the national consciousness of the German people. He not only accurately reflected the mentality of his time but actually did much to shape it.

[28] Crane Brinton, "Natural Rights," *E.S.S.,* Vol. VI.

[29] *Ibid.*

[30] *Ibid.*

[31] "Two Treatises of Government," *The Works of John Locke* (12th ed., 1824). Vol. IV. Bk. II, ch. ii, sec. 6. Locke regarded property as an essential attribute of personality. See Bk. II, ch. v. The ideal of laissez-faire philosophy was economic democracy.

[32] *Ibid.*

[33] See Locke, *op. cit.*, Bk. II, ch. xix, sec. 221.

[34] See Brinton, *op. cit.*

[35] Rousseau, *The Social Contract* (translated by H. J. Tozer, 3d ed., 1902), Bk. I, ch. iv. Italics mine.

[36] Quoted by Fritz Berolzheimer, *The World's Legal Philosophies* (translated by R. S. Jastrow, 1912), p. 160.

[37] Christian Wolff, *Jus naturae methodo scientifica pertractatum* (1740–1749), Part I, pars. 23 ff, 64, 72; chs. ii–iv. Quoted by Berolzheimer, *ibid.*, p. 161.

[38] Humboldt, *op. cit.*, p. 107.

[39] Fichte, *op. cit.*, p. 94.

[40] *Loc. cit.*

[41] Voltaire, *Pensées sur l'administration publique.* Quoted by Hermann Heller, *Europa und der Fascismus* (2d ed., 1931), p. 17.

[42] As one writer states this view: " ... the real problem is not that of arriving at an organization of society and the state under which these two would grant freedom to human personality, but rather the problem of confirming the freedom of the personality against the unlimited authority of society and the state. This means that true freedom has a spiritual rather than a social origin; it is defined by its being rooted in the spiritual rather than the social world." Nicholas Berdyaev, *The Fate of Man in the Modern World* (translated by D. A. Lowrie, 1935), p. 42.

[43] Grotius, *De Jure Belli ac Pacis* (Whewell's ed., 1853), Bk. I, ch. i, sec. 10. A similar idea had already been expressed by Gabriel Biel in the fifteenth century when he wrote: "si per impossibile deus non esset, qui est ratio divina, aut ratio illa divina esset errans: adhuc si quis ageret contra rectam rationem angelicam vel humanam aut aliam aliquam, si qua esset—peccaret . . . " Quoted by Wilhelm Dilthey, "Weltanschauung und Analyse des Menschen seit Renaissance und Reformation," *Gesammelte Schriften*, Vol. II, p. 279, note 1.

[44] Grotius, *op. cit.*, *Prolegomena*, sec. 16.

[45] *Ibid.*, secs. 9–11.

[46] Reinhold Aris, *History of Political Thought in Germany from 1789 to 1815* (1936), p. 70.

[47] Roscoe Pound, "Jurisprudence," *E.S.S.*, Vol. IV.

[48] *Ibid.*

[49] Jean Bodin, *Les Six Livres de la République* (1583), Bk. I, ch. viii.

[50] See Shepard's article, "Sovereignty at the Crossroads," *Political Science Quarterly* (1930), pp. 580 ff.

[51] Quoted by Shepard, *op. cit.*, p. 582.

[52] Bodin, *op. cit.*, Bk. I, ch. viii.

[53] Locke, *op. cit.*, Bk. II, ch. xi, sec. 135.

[54] *Ibid.*, ch. xviii, sec. 202.

[55] Quoted by Gide and Rist, *op. cit.*, p. 8.

[56] *Loc. cit.*

[57] Gide and Rist, *op. cit.*, pp. 9–10.

[58] Horton, *op. cit.*, p. 82.

[59] Quoted by Gide and Rist, *op. cit.*, p. 93.

[60] Humboldt was born in 1767 and died in 1835. The *Ideen* was published posthumously in Berlin in 1851. It had been written originally in 1791. Humboldt served for a year (1790–1791) on the High Court in Berlin. He resigned the post and spent the next ten years traveling and writing. He was an intimate friend of Schiller, Goethe, and Wolff, and moved about in the best intellectual and social circles. In 1802 he was sent as Prussian ambassador to the Papal Court in Rome where he stayed for six years. In 1808 he became Prussian minister of worship and public instruction, an appointment which was curious enough since he had opposed in his earlier writings any state solicitude for religion or education. The ministry was abolished in 1810 but Humboldt was instrumental in founding the University of Berlin. He was appointed ambassador to Austria, attended the Congress of Vienna, and in

1818 became Prussian minister of the interior. Strongly opposing the Carlsbad decrees and constantly urging the establishment of constitutional government, he made himself unpopular with his ministerial colleagues, as well as with the cabinets in Vienna and Petersburg, and finally resigned his post to retire on a pension.

[61] Humboldt, *op. cit.*, p. 3.

[62] *Loc. cit.*

[63] Humboldt, *op. cit.*, p. 17.

[64] *Ibid.*, p. 18.

[65] *Ibid.*, p. 19.

[66] *Loc. cit.*

[67] Humboldt, *op. cit.*, p. 15.

[68] *Ibid.*, p. 20.

[69] *Ibid.*, p. 22.

[70] *Ibid.*, p. 23.

[71] *Ibid.*, p. 39.

[72] *Ibid.*, p. 46.

[73] *Ibid.*, p. 45.

[74] *Ibid.*, p. 75.

[75] *Ibid.*, p. 82.

[76] *Ibid.*, p. 101.

[77] See *ibid.*, p. 105, and ch. xiv.

[78] *Ibid.*, p. 103.

[79] As Hermann Heller describes this notion of law: "Unter Gesetz aber versteht man je länger je mehr nicht den Willen eines personlichen Gottes oder gottbegnadeten Monarchen, sondern die über alle Willen und jedwede Willkur erhabene Norm; den Inhalt dieser Gesetze will man in zunehmenden Masse aus dem diesseitigen und vernünftig erkennbaren Sein von Natur und Gesellschaft ablesen." *Rechtsstaat oder Diktatur?* (1930), p. 7.

[80] C. H. McIlwain, "The Fundamental Law behind the Constitution of the United States," in Conyers Read (ed.), *The Constitution Reconsidered* (1938), p. 3.

[81] *Loc. cit.*

[82] McIlwain, *op cit.*, p. 7.

[83] Bracton, *De Legibus et Consuetudinibus Angliae* (Twiss, ed., 1854), f. 5b. Quoted by E. S. Corwin, "The 'Higher Law' Background of American Constitutional Law," *Harvard Law Review* (1928), Vol. 42, pp. 149–185, 365–409.

[84] McIlwain, *op. cit.*, p. 5.

[85] *Loc. cit.*

[86] Fichte, *op. cit.*, p. 103.

[87] *Loc. cit.*

[88] Fichte, *op. cit.*, p. 104.

[89] *Ibid.*, p. 105.

[90] *Ibid.*, p. 106.

[91] See *ibid.*, pp. 106 ff.

[92] *Ibid.*, p. 106, *et passim*.

[93] *Ibid.*, pp. 108–109.

[94] *Ibid.*, p. 109.

[95] See *ibid.*, p. 159.

[96] See *ibid.*, pp. 160 ff.

[97] F. W. Kaufmann, "Fichte and National Socialism," *American Political Science Review* (June, 1942), p. 460.

[98] *Ibid.*, p. 470.

[99] Giuseppe Mazzini, *The Duties of Man* (1858). Quoted by Irwin Edman, *Fountainheads of Freedom* (1941), pp. 512–513.

[100] *Ibid.*, p. 517.

[101] Otto Bähr, *Der Rechtsstaat: Eine Publicistische Skizze* (1864), p. 8.

[102] Rudolph von Gneist, *Zur Verwaltungsreform und Verwaltungsrechtspflege in Preussen* (1880), p. 50.

[103] See *idem, Der Rechtsstaat* (1872).

[104] See Robert von Mohl, "Gesellschaftswissenschaft und Staatswissenschaft," *Zeitschrift für die gesammte Staatswissenschaft* (1851), Vol. 7; Lorenz von Stein, *System der Staatswissenschaft* (1856); and *idem, Der Begriff der Gesellschaft* (1855).

NOTES TO CHAPTER III

THE INFLUENCE OF HISTORICISM AND POSITIVISM UPON ORIGINAL LIBERAL CONCEPTS

[1] Ernst Troeltsch, "The Ideas of Natural Law and Humanity," in Otto Gierke, *Natural Law and the Theory of Society 1500 to 1800* (translated by Ernest Barker, 1934), p. 211.

[2] *Loc. cit.*

[3] *Loc. cit.*

[4] Troeltsch, *op. cit.*, p. 213.

[5] *Ibid.*, p. 218.

[6] A. N. Whitehead, *Science and the Modern World* (1925).

[7] E. S. Corwin, "The 'Higher Law' Background of American Constitutional Law," *Harvard Law Review*, Vol. 42 (1928), p. 382, note 59.

[8] *Ibid.*, p. 408.

[9] E. B. Ashton, *The Fascist: His State and His Mind* (1937), p. 127.

[10] *Ibid.*, p. 132.

[11] *Ibid.*, p. 133.

[12] Nicholas Berdyaev, *The Fate of Man in the Modern World* (1935), p. 46.

[13] *Ibid.*, p. 44.

[14] When contemporary "liberals" talk about the rule of reason they tend to forget this. It is frequently suggested that difficulties between various interest groups, between capital and labor for example, could be solved if only they would agree to sit around a conference table and confer as "reasonable" men. This would only provide a solution, however, if the conferees agreed to reason from the same premises and to accept the same set of values. Reasoning from different premises they would arrive at equally reasonable but widely divergent conclusions.

[15] Roscoe Pound, *Interpretations of Legal History* (1923), pp. 9–10.

[16] *Ibid.*, p. 11.

[17] *Ibid.*, p. 12.

[18] Roscoe Pound, *The Spirit of the Common Law* (1921), p. 142.

[19] *Ibid.*, p. 143.

[20] F. K. Savigny, *Of the Vocation of Our Age for Legislation and Jurisprudence* (translated by A. Hayward, 1831), p. 30.

[21] *Ibid.*, p. 24.

[22] N. M. Korkunov, *General Theory of Law* (translated by W. G. Hastings, 1909), pp. 120–121.

[23] Immanuel Kant, *Metaphysische Anfangsgründe der Rechtslehre* (K. Vorländer, ed., 1907), Introduction, paragraphs *A, B*.

[24] Pound, *Spirit of the Common Law*, pp. 151–152.

[25] *Ibid.*, pp. 153–154.

[26] Pound, *Interpretations of Legal History*, p. 98.

[27] C. F. Puchta, *Outlines of Jurisprudence as the Science of Right—A Juristic Encyclopedia* (translated by W. Hastie, 1887), p. 26.

[28] *Ibid.*, pp. 30–31.

[29] Max Lerner, "Social Process," *E.S.S.*, Vol. VII.

[30] *Ibid.*

[31] Hegel, *Grundlinien der Philosophie des Rechts* (1821), sec. 278.

[32] Rupert Emerson, *State and Sovereignty in Modern Germany* (1928), p. 14.

[33] A. N. Whitehead, *Adventures of Ideas* (1933), p. 41.

[34] *Ibid.*, p. 45.

[35] *Loc. cit.*

[36] "Society," *E.S.S.*, Vol. VII.

[37] Jhering, *Law as a Means to an End* (translated by I. Husik, 1913), p. liv.

[38] *Ibid.*, p. 242.

[39] *Ibid.*, p. 380.

[40] *Ibid.*, p. 239.

[41] *Ibid.*, p. 73.

[42] *Loc. cit.*

[43] Jhering, *op. cit.*, p. 404.

[44] *Ibid.*, p. 28.

[45] Guido de Ruggiero, "Positivism," *E.S.S.*, Vol. VI.

[46] *Loc. cit.*

[47] *Loc. cit.*

[48] Science, as Whitehead has so well stated, rests in the last analysis upon an "instinctive faith that there is an Order of Nature which can be traced in every detailed occurrence." He goes on to say that we all share this faith and "believe that the reason for the faith is our apprehension of its truth. But the formation of a general idea—such as the idea of the Order of Nature—and the grasp of its importance, and the observation of its exemplification in a variety of occasions are by no means the necessary consequences of the truth of the idea in question." *Science and the Modern World*, p. 6. See also J. W. N. Sullivan, *The Limitations of Science* (1933), and Wolfgang Köhler, *The Place of Value in a World of Facts* (1938).

[49] Whitehead, *Adventures of Ideas*, p. 147.

[50] *Ibid.*, p. 159.

[51] *Ibid.*, p. 157.

[52] See Fritz Berolzheimer, *The World's Legal Philosophies* (translated by R. S. Jastrow, 1912), pp. 308 ff.

NOTES TO CHAPTER IV

FORMAL LIBERALISM

[1] Paul Tillich, *The Religious Situation* (translated by R. Niebuhr, 1932), p. 108.

[2] *Loc. cit.*

[3] Tillich, *op cit.*, p. 136.

[4] *Ibid.*, pp. 19–20.

[5] *Ibid.*, p. 20.

[6] *Ibid.*, p. 90.

[7] Nicholas Berdyaev, *The Fate of Man in the Modern World* (translated by D. A. Lowrie, 1935), p. 46.

[8] See Max Weber, *The Protestant Ethic and the Spirit of Capitalism* (translated by Talcott Parsons, 1930).

[9] Berdyaev, *op. cit.*, p. 43.

[10] *Loc. cit.*

[11] Quoted by Hermann Heller, *Die politischen Ideenkrise der Gegenwart* (1926), p. 69.

[12] Berdyaev, *op. cit.*, p. 43.

[13] Brinton, "Natural Rights," *E.S.S.*, Vol. VI.

[14] Adam Smith, *The Theory of Moral Sentiments* (1st American ed., 1817), p. 134.

[15] *Ibid.*, p. 382.

[16] *Ibid.*, p. 557, *et passim*. Italics mine.

[17] Roscoe Pound, *The Spirit of the Common Law* (1921), p. 161.

[18] *Ibid.*, pp. 161–162.

[19] *Ibid.*, pp. 162–163.

[20] *Ibid.*, p. 163.

[21] *Ibid.*, p. 164.

[22] *Loc. cit.*

[23] Pound, *op. cit.*, pp. 163–164.

[24] See chapter i, above.

[25] Hermann Heller, *Rechtsstaat oder Diktatur?* (1930).

[26] C. F. von Gerber, *Grundzüge eines Systems des deutschen Staatsrechts* (1865), p. 3.

[27] *Ibid.*, p. 4.

[28] *Ibid.*, p. 19.

[29] *Ibid.*, p. 19, note 1.

[30] Here in Gerber is the suggestion that will may be separated from norm, fact from standard. It is the introduction of this duality into jurisprudence that made possible the thought of Kelsen, on the one hand, and Carl Schmitt, on the other. At the turn of the century there was no other logical possibility but to make one or the other absolute.

[31] Gerber, *op. cit.*, p. 29.

[32] Paul Laband, *Das Staatsrecht des deutschen Reiches* (5th ed., 4 vols., 1911–1914), Vol. II, p. 4.

[33] *Ibid.*, pp. 29–30.

[34] Philipp Zorn, *Das Staatsrecht des deutschen Reiches* (1880), Vol. I, pp. 111–112.

[35] Laband, *op. cit.*, Vol. II, p. 186.

[36] Laband, *Deutsches Reichsstaatsrecht* (1907), p. 17.

[37] Georg Jellinek, *Allgemeine Staatslehre* (3d ed., 1914), p. 386.

[38] *Ibid.*, pp. 481–482.

[39] *Ibid.*, p. 482. Italics mine.

[40] H. E. Cohen, *Recent Theories of Sovereignty* (1937), p. 144.

[41] Jellinek, *System der subjektiven öffentlichen Rechte* (1905), p. 17.

[42] *Ibid.*, p. 225.

[43] Cf., Heinrich Triepel, *Völkerrecht und Landesrecht* (1899), p. 78.

[44] Cf., Albert Haenel, *Gesetz im formellen und materiellen Sinne* (1888), p. 231.

[45] Kurt Pfeifer, *Die Idee der Grundrechte in der deutschen Literatur von 1790 bis Georg Jellinek (1890)* (1930).

[46] Jellinek, *System der subjektiven öffentlichen Rechte*, p. 82.

[47] *Loc. cit.*

[48] *Loc. cit.* Italics mine.

[49] Jellinek, *System der subjektiven öffentlichen Rechte*, pp. 103 ff.

[50] *Ibid.*, p. 103.

[51] Cf., *ibid.*, pp. 329 ff.

[52] Cf., *ibid.*, pp. 53 ff., 68 ff., 114 ff., and 234 ff.

[53] *Ibid.*, p. 53.

[54] Hermann Heller, "Der Begriff des Gesetzes in der Reichsverfassung," *Veröffentlichungen der Vereinigung der deutschen Staatsrechtslehrer* (Heft 4, 1928), p. 116.

[55] Quoted by Heller, *ibid.*, p. 112.

NOTES TO CHAPTER V

BEYOND GOOD AND EVIL

[1] C. E. M. Joad, *Guide to Philosophy* (1936), p. 496.

[2] Quoted by Joad, *loc. cit.*

[3] Joad, *op. cit.*, p. 532.

[4] *Ibid.*, p. 452.

[5] This philosophy finds expression in America in the well-known writings of William James and Charles Peirce. In Germany, where it is known as the "Philosophy of 'as if'," its leading exponent was Hans Vaihinger (1852–1933).

[6] Joad, *op. cit.*, p. 464.

[7] *Loc. cit.* Italics mine.

[8] From a speech delivered by Ernst Krieck, now Rector of Heidelberg University, upon the occasion of the celebration in July, 1936 of the 550th anniversary of the founding of the university.

[9] In somewhat abstract terms Bott-Bodenhausen explains how will (*Individualismus*) and norm (*Substantialismus*) were bound together as complementary elements before their separation by positivism. He writes: "Auf dem Rechtsgebiet . . . haben Substantialismus und Individualismus sich zu einer Verbindung verhäkelt. Diese Verbindung ist der Formativismus. Er ist keine innere Verschmelzung, sondern eine äussere Angleichung. Bald überwiegt in

diesem Gestaltssystem das substantielle, bald das individuelle Moment. Stets aber treten beide gleichzeitig in die Erscheinung, findet das Individualistische sein Mass in einem Seienden, erhält ein Seiendes seinen Impuls durch ein Individuelles." Manfred Bott-Bodenhausen, *Formatives und funktionales Recht in der gegenwärtigen Kulturkrisis* (1926), p. 22.

Kelsen declares: "The contrast between Is and Ought is formal and logical and as long as one keeps within the limits of formal and logical considerations no road leads from one to the other; the two worlds confronting each other are separated by an unbridgeable gulf. Logically the question as to the 'why' of some particular Ought can only lead to some other Ought, time and again, just as the question as to the 'why' of some Is can only receive as an answer another Is, time and again." *Ueber Grenzen Zwischen Juristischer und Soziologisicher Methode* (1911), p. 6, quoted by Arnold Brecht, "The Myth of *Is* and *Ought*," *Harvard Law Review*, March, 1941, pp. 811–831.

[10] Rudolph Stammler, "Fundamental Tendencies in Modern Jurisprudence," *Michigan Law Review*, Vol. 21 (1923), pp. 862 ff.

[11] *Ibid.*

[12] Stammler, *Theorie der Rechtswissenschaft* (1911), p. 17. Italics mine.

[13] Rupert Emerson, *State and Sovereignty in Modern Germany* (1928), p. 163.

[14] Stammler, "Fundamental Tendencies . . . ," p. 863.

[15] *Loc. cit.*

[16] Morris Ginsberg, "Stammler's Philosophy of Law," in *Modern Theories of Law* (1933), pp. 40–41.

[17] Quoted by Ginsberg, *ibid.*, p. 42.

[18] Stammler, *The Theory of Justice* (translated by I. Husik, 1925), p. 40.

[19] *Ibid.*, p. 89.

[20] See Emerson, *op. cit.*, p. 165.

[21] Stammler, "Fundamental Tendencies . . ." p. 865.

[22] *Ibid.*

[23] *Ibid.*

[24] Emerson, *op. cit.*, p. 164.

[25] Ginsberg, *op. cit.*, p. 45. Since Stammler's "idea of justice" is purely formal and without any substantive content it provides no criteria for obligation. Moral obligation is only possible where certain objective values are conceived as existing. Obligation means that you ought or ought not to will *something;* hence, you have to know *what* it is you ought or ought not to will. A formal "idea of justice" without substantive content doesn't tell you this.

[26] See Stammler's *Wirtschaft und Recht nach der materialistischen Geschichtsauffassung* (3d ed., 1914), p. 554.

[27] Stammler, *Theorie der Rechtswissenschaft*, p. 27.

[28] W. E. Hocking, *Present Status of the Philosophy of Law and of Rights* (1926), pp. 16–17.

[29] *Ibid.*, p. 17.

[30] *Ibid.*, p. 18.

[31] Erich Kaufmann, *Kritik der neukantischen Rechtsphilosophie* (1921), p. 20.

[32] Emerson, *op. cit.*, pp. 168–169.

[33] Hans Kelsen, "Centralization and Decentralization" (translated by W. Kraus), in *Authority and the Individual* (1937), p. 212.

[34] *Ibid.*, p. 213.

[35] *Loc. cit.*

[36] *Loc. cit.*

[37] *Loc. cit.*

[38] Hans Lauterpacht, "Kelsen's Pure Science of Law," *Modern Theories of Law,* pp. 111–112.

[39] Kelsen, "The Pure Theory of Law" (translated by C. H. Wilson), *Law Quarterly Review,* Vol. 51 (1935), pp. 517 ff. Italics mine.

[40] *Ibid.* Italics mine.

[41] *Ibid.*

[42] Emerson, *op. cit.,* pp. 170–171.

[43] Kelsen, *Hauptprobleme der Staatsrechtslehre* (1911), p. 465. Quoted by Emerson, *op. cit.,* p. 171.

[44] Adolf Lasson, *System der Rechtsphilosophie* (1882), p. viii.

[45] Quoted by Emerson, *op. cit.,* p. 187.

[46] Lasson, *op. cit.,* p. 288.

[47] *Ibid.,* pp. 289–290.

[48] Quoted by Hocking, *op. cit.,* p. 25.

[49] Kohler, *Moderne Rechtsprobleme,* p. 11. Quoted by Hocking, *op. cit.,* p. 32.

[50] Kohler, *Philosophy of Law* (translated by A. Albrecht, 1914), pp. 208–209, 241–242.

[51] *Ibid.,* p. 59.

[52] *Ibid.,* p. 208.

[53] *Ibid.,* p. 253.

[54] Quoted by Hocking, *op. cit.,* p. 8.

[55] Kohler, *Philosophy of Law,* p. 36.

[56] Hocking, *op. cit.,* p. 26.

[57] *Ibid.,* p. 30.

[58] Emerson, *op. cit.,* p. 199.

[59] See Fritz Berolzheimer, *The World's Legal Philosophies* (translated by R. S. Jastrow, 1912), pp. 466 ff.

[60] Erich Kaufmann, *Das Wesen des Völkerrechts und die Clausala rebus sic stantibus* (1911), p. 138.

[61] *Ibid.,* p. 135.

[62] Cf. *ibid.,* pp. 151–152.

[63] Carl Schmitt, *Der Begriff des Politischen* (3d ed., 1933).

[64] Aurel Kolnai, *The War Against the West* (1938), p. 143, *et passim.*

[65] Schmitt, *Verfassungslehre* (1928), ch. iii.

[66] *Ibid.*

[67] Quoted by Hermann Heller, *Staatslehre* (1934), p. 221.

NOTES TO CHAPTER VI

FROM NIHILISM TO TYRANNY

[1] Gerhart Niemeyer observes: " . . . the two ways of legal thinking, the 'essential' and the 'personalistic' approach, represent two systems of theory, each complete in itself, based on its own premises and proceeding with its own peculiar ideas. Neither of these theoretical systems needs the other one; they are self-sufficient and logically incompatible with each other. One starts from the fact of the existence of the individual person, the other starts out from the idea of order of the creation. One takes it to be the irrational impulse of

personal interests which drives the individual to consent to legal rules, the other construes law as the consequence of absolute values which force themselves upon the recognition of all human beings ... torn and undecided between two eras, the seventeenth-century mind had to merge the mediaeval idea of an absolute order as the essence of reality with the Renaissance conception of the individual person as the ultimately moving force in legal order. The merger ... was not dictated by logical necessity, but by emotional forces which, though conflicting, coincided in the mentality of the seventeenth century." *Law Without Force: The Function of Politics in International Law* (1941), pp. 145–146. See ch. iv of this work for a more complete discussion of this point.

[2] See the preceding chapter for a more complete analysis.

[3] " ... a moment has come when the civilized world, in relation to the capacity of the average man, has taken on an appearance of superabundance, of excess of riches, of superfluity. A single example of this: the security seemingly offered by progress (i.e., the ever-growing increase of vital advantages) demoralized the average man, inspiring him with a confidence which is false, vicious, and atrophying." Ortega y Gasset, *The Revolt of the Masses* (1932), p. 110, footnote 1.

[4] Paul Tillich, *The Religious Situation* (translated by Reinhold Niebuhr, 1932).

[5] See preceding chapter. Today "when German judges [trained in the liberal tradition] adjudicate ... 'in National Socialist spirit,' to the extent of twisting the letter of existing precepts, this is no mere subservience to a political upheaval but an earnest and sincere fulfillment of judicial duty as it is now conceived" states E. B. Ashton, *The Fascist: His State and His Mind* (1937), p. 131. He continues: " ... the vast majority of the highly conscientious and professionally proud German civil servants adjusted themselves to the new doctrine with surprising ease. ... As a matter of fact, what we call 'misapplying the law,' to the Fascist simply means applying it in accordance with the principles that made it law. As a great German jurist put it: 'The will of the State is the soul of the law.'" *Ibid*, p. 132. Positivist "liberal" jurists had been expounding the principle that "the will of the State is the soul of the law" for many years prior to 1933. This was no new idea. The National Socialist simply took over the positivist "liberal" doctrine that law is the command of superior force.

[6] Hermann Heller, *Europa und der Fascismus*, 2d ed. (1931), p. 18.

[7] *Ibid.*, p. 20.

[8] " ... when the humanists appeared upon the scene, with their Gospel of salvation by scientific research and coöperative effort, the dilemma of liberalism became acute. The humanists professed to be the real moderns, and it must be admitted that their position represented, in some respects, a logically consequent outworking of principles to which liberals themselves had appealed in their critique of fundamentalism. ... Was there in fact any shore to which they could return, now that they had cut loose from churchly tradition and infallible revelation, and committed themselves to the outcome of free inquiry, whatever it might be?" W. M. Horton, *Realistic Theology* (1934), pp. 3–4.

[9] *Ibid.*, pp. 37–38.

[10] Niemeyer, *op. cit.*, p. 199.

[11] Lewis Mumford, *Faith for Living* (1940), pp. 88–89. "The upshot of this argument is simple. Good and evil are real, as virtue and sin are real. Evil is not just a mental aberration, which pathological characters are the victims

of; and sin is not just a symptom of mental immaturity as the pragmatic liberal would have it. Both these optimistic interpretations of sin and evil lead always to the flattering conclusion that the intelligent cannot sin and that the mentally adult can do no evil. These conclusions are plainly gratifying to those who fancy themselves intelligent and mature, because it leads them to a super-Calvinistic state of grace, in which all things are possible, and whatever one does is blessed. At that point, the pragmatic liberal and the fascist meet face to face. And whatever the fascist's contempt for the liberal, there is plenty of evidence at hand to prove that the liberal, face to face with fascism, can literally not find words to condemn it. This refusal to recognize evil as evil has fatally delayed the world's reaction against barbarism." *Ibid.*, pp. 82.

And Reinhold Niebuhr declares:
"The utopian illusions and sentimental aberrations of modern liberal culture are really all derived from the basic error of negating the fact of original sin. This error ... continually betrays modern man to equate the goodness of men with the virtue of their various schemes for social justice and international peace. When these schemes fail of realization or are realized only after tragic conflicts, modern men either turn from utopianism to disillusionment and despair, or they seek to place the onus of their failure upon some particular social group or upon some particular form of economic and social organization.

"Obviously there are varying degrees of sin and guilt and some men and nations are more guilty than others of 'disobedience to the heavenly vision.' Also there are specific evils in history, arising from specific maladjustments in social and political organization. But these evils can be dealt with most adequately, if men do not give themselves to the illusion that some particular organization of society might be found in which men would no longer stand in contradiction to the law of their own being. Furthermore, particular virulent forms and types of sin in particular men and nations can be checked most successfully if it is recognized that these types are but aggravations of a general human situation.

"Both modern liberalism and modern Marxism are always facing the alternatives of moral futility or moral fanaticism. Liberalism in its pure form usually succumbs to the peril of futility. It will not act against evil until it is able to find a vantage point of guiltlessness from which to operate. This means that it cannot act at all. Sometimes it imagines that this inaction is the guiltlessness for which it has been seeking. A minority of liberals and most of the Marxists solve the problem by assuming that they have found a position of guiltlessness in action. Thereby they are betrayed into the error of fanaticism. The whole history of modern culture, particularly in its more recent efforts to defend itself against inferior and more demonic cultures, is a pathetic revelation of the weakness and confusion which result from these illusions about the character of man." *The Nature and Destiny of Man* (1941), Vol. I, p. 273, footnote 4.

[12] Aurel Kolnai, *The War Against the West* (1938), p. 15.

[13] Hermann Rauschning, *The Revolution of Nihilism: Warning to the West* (1939).

[14] Stephen Raushenbush, *The March of Fascism* (1939), ch. vii.

[15] Peter Drucker, *The End of Economic Man: A Study of the New Totalitarianism* (1939), pp. 227 ff.

[16] Oswald Spengler, *Politische Schriften* (1934), pp. 85–86. Quoted by Melvin Rader, *No Compromise: The Conflict between Two Worlds* (1939), p. 304.

BIBLIOGRAPHY

SELECT BIBLIOGRAPHY

ARIS, REINHOLD. *History of Political Thought in Germany from 1789 to 1815* (London: Allen and Unwin, 1936). 414 pp.

ASHTON, E. B. *The Fascist: His State and His Mind* (New York: Morrow, 1937). 320 pp.

BÄHR, OTTO. *Der Rechtsstaat: eine publicistische Skizze* (Cassel: Wigand, 1864). 194 pp.

BERDYAEV, NICHOLAS. *The Fate of Man in the Modern World,* translated by D. A. Lowrie (London: Student Christian Movement Press, 1935). 131 pp.

BEROLZHEIMER, FRITZ. *The World's Legal Philosophies,* translated by R. S. Jastrow (Boston: Boston Book Co., 1912). 490 pp.

BODIN, JEAN. *Les Six Livres de la République* (Paris: Iacques du Puys, 1583). 1104 pp.

BOTT-BODENHAUSEN, MANFRED. *Formatives und funktionales Recht in der gegenwärtigen Kulturkrisis* (Berlin-Grunewald: Rothschild, 1926).

BRECHT, ARNOLD. "The Myth of *Is* and *Ought,*" *Harvard Law Review* (March, 1941), pp. 811–831.

BREDT, J. V. *Der Geist der deutschen Reichsverfassung* (Berlin: Stilke, 1924). 465 pp.

BRINTON, CRANE. *The Anatomy of Revolution* (New York: Norton, 1938). 326 pp.

BRUCK, W. F. *Social and Economic History of Germany from William II to Hitler 1888–1938* (London: Oxford University Press, 1938). 291 pp.

COHEN, H. E. *Recent Theories of Sovereignty* (Chicago: University of Chicago Press, 1937). 169 pp.

CORWIN, E. S. "The 'Higher Law' Background of American Constitutional Law," *Harvard Law Review,* Vol. XLII (1928), 149–185, 365–409.

DILTHEY, WILHELM. "Weltanschauung und Analyse des Menschen seit Renaissance und Reformation," *Gesammelte Schriften* (Leipzig: Teubner, 1914). Vol. II.

DRUCKER, P. F. *The End of Economic Man: A Study of the New Totalitarianism* (New York: John Day, 1939). 268 pp.

EDMAN, IRWIN. *Fountainheads of Freedom: The Growth of the Democratic Idea* (New York: Reynal and Hitchcock, 1941). 576 pp.

EINSTEIN, ALBERT, and INFELD, LEOPOLD. *The Evolution of Physics: The Growth of Ideas from Early Concepts to Relativity and Quanta* (New York: Simon and Schuster, 1938). 319 pp.

EMERSON, RUPERT. *State and Sovereignty in Modern Germany* (New Haven: Yale University Press, 1928). 282 pp.

ERMARTH, FRITZ. *The New Germany: National Socialist Government in Theory and Practice* (Washington: Digest Press, 1936). 203 pp.

FICHTE, J. G. "Grundlage des Naturrechts nach Principien der Wissenschaftslehre," in *Sämmtliche Werke* (Berlin: Veit, 1845). Vol. III, 8 vols.

GERBER, C. F. VON. *Grundzüge eines Systems des deutschen Staatsrechts* (Leipzig: Tauchnitz, 1865). 264 pp.

GIDE, CHARLES, and RIST, CHARLES. *A History of Economic Doctrines from the Time of the Physiocrats to the Present Day*, translated by R. Richards (New York: Heath, 1916). 672 pp.

GIERKE, OTTO VON. *Johannes Althusius und die Entwicklung der naturrechtlichen Staatstheorien* (4th ed.; Breslau: Marcus, 1929). 366 pp.

———. *Natural Law and the Theory of Society 1500 to 1800*, with a lecture on "The Ideas of Natural Law and Humanity," by Ernst Troeltsch, translated with an introduction by Ernest Barker (Cambridge, England: University Press, 1934). 2 vols.

GNEIST, RUDOLPH VON. *Der Rechtsstaat* (Berlin: Springer, 1872). 202 pp.

———. *Zur Verwaltungsreform und Verwaltungsrechtspflege in Preussen* (Leipzig: Brockhaus, 1880). 76 pp.

GROTIUS, HUGO. *De Jure Belli ac Pacis*, edited by Whewell (Cambridge, England: University Press, 1853). 3 vols.

HAENEL, ALBERT. *Studien zum deutschen Staatsrecht* (Leipzig: Haessel, 1873–1888). 2 vols.

HAINES, C. G. *The Revival of Natural Law Concepts* (Cambridge: Harvard University Press, 1930). 388 pp.

HARVARD, UNIVERSITY. *Authority and the Individual* (Cambridge: Harvard University Press, Tercentenary Publication, 1937). 371 pp.

HEGEL, G. W. F. *Grundlinien der Philosophie des Rechts* (Berlin: Nicolai, 1821).

HELLER, HERMANN. *Die politischen Ideenkrise der Gegenwart* (Breslau: Hirt, 1926). 156 pp.

———. *Die Souveränität: ein Beitrag zur Theorie des Staats- und Völkerrechts* (Berlin: Gruyter, 1927). 177 pp.

———. "Der Begriff des Gesetzes in der Reichsverfassung," *Veröffentlichungen der Vereinigung der deutschen Staatsrechtslehrer*, Heft 4 (1928).

———. *Rechtsstaat oder Diktatur?* (Tübingen: Mohr, 1930). 26 pp.

———. *Europa und der Fascismus* (2d ed.; Berlin: Gruyter, 1931). 159 pp.

———. *Staatslehre*, edited by Gerhart Niemeyer (Leiden: Sijthoff, 1934). 298 pp.

HOCKING, W. E. *Present Status of the Philosophy of Law and of Rights* (New Haven: Yale University Press, 1926). 97 pp.

HORTON, W. M. *Realistic Theology* (New York: Harper, 1934). 207 pp.

JELLINEK, GEORG. *Allgemeine Staatslehre* (3d ed.; Berlin: Häring, 1914). 837 pp.

———. *System der subjektiven öffentlichen Rechte* (2d ed.; Tübingen: Mohr, 1905). 366 pp.

JHERING, RUDOLPH VON. *Law as a Means to an End*, translated by Isaac Husik (Boston: Boston Book Co., 1913). 483 pp.

JOAD, C. E. M. *Guide to Philosophy* (New York: Random House, 1936). 592 pp.

KANT, IMMANUEL. *Grundlegung zur Metaphysik der Sitten*, edited by Roudolph Otto (Gotha: Klotz, 1930). 213 pp.

KAUFMANN, ERICH. *Kritik der neukantischen Rechtsphilosophie* (Tübingen: Mohr, 1921). 102 pp.

————. *Das Wesen des Völkerrechts und die Clausala rebus sic stantibus* (Tübingen: Mohr, 1911). 231 pp.

KAUFMANN, F. W. "Fichte and National Socialism," *American Political Science Review* (June, 1942), pp. 460 ff.

KELSEN, HANS. *Allgemeine Staatslehre* (Berlin: Springer, 1925). 433 pp.

————. "The Pure Theory of Law," translated by C. H. Wilson, *Law Quarterly Review*, Vol. LI (1935), pp. 517 ff.

KÖHLER, J. P. "Staat und Gesellschaft in der deutschen Theorie der auswärtigen Wirtschaftspolitik und des internationalen Handels von Schlettwein bis auf Fr. List und Prince-Smith," *Beihefte zur Vierteljahrschrift für Sozial- und Wirtschaftsgeschichte*, Heft VII (1926).

KÖHLER, WOLFGANG. *The Place of Value in a World of Facts* (New York: Liveright, 1938). 418 pp.

KOHLER, JOSEF. *Philosophy of Law*, translated by Albert Albrecht (Boston: Boston Book Co., 1914). 390 pp.

KOLNAI, AUREL. *The War Against the West* (London: Gollancz, 1938). 711 pp.

KORKUNOV, N. M. *General Theory of Law*, translated by W. G. Hastings (Boston: Boston Book Co., 1909). 524 pp.

LABAND, PAUL. *Deutsches Reichsstaatsrecht* (Tübingen: Mohr, 1907). 448 pp.

————. *Das Staatsrecht des deutschen Reiches* (4th ed.; Tübingen: Mohr, 1901). 4 vols.

LASKI, H. J. *The Rise of Liberalism: the Philosophy of a Business Civilization* (New York: Harper's, 1936). 327 pp.

LASSON, ADOLF. *System der Rechtsphilosophie* (Berlin: Guttentag, 1882) 708 pp.

LAUN, RUDOLPH. *Der Wandel der Ideen Staat und Volk als Aeusserung des Weltgewissens* (Barcelona: Elzeviriana, 1933). 463 pp.

LIPPMANN, WALTER. *An Inquiry into the Principles of the Good Society* (Boston: Little, Brown; 1937). 402 pp.

LOCKE, JOHN. *The Works of John Locke* (12th ed.; London: C. and J. Rivington, 1824). 9 vols.

MACKINTOSH, H. R. *Types of Modern Theology: Schleiermacher to Barth* (London: Nisbet, 1937). 333 pp.

MANNHEIM, KARL. *Ideology and Utopia*, translated by L. Wirth and E. Shils (New York: Harcourt, Brace, 1936). 318 pp.

MARCK, SIEGFRIED. *Substanz- und Funktionsbegriff in der Rechtsphilosophie* (Tübingen: Mohr, 1925). 156 pp.

MEINECKE, FRIEDRICH. *Die Idee der Staatsräson in der neueren Geschichte* (Munich: Oldenbourg, 1924). 545 pp.

MERRIAM, C. E., and BARNES, H. E. (editors). *A History of Political Theories: Recent Times* (New York: Macmillan, 1924). 597 pp.

Modern Theories of Law (London: Oxford University Press, 1933). 229 pp.

MOHL, ROBERT VON. "Gesellschaftswissenschaft und Staatswissenschaft," *Zeitschrift für die gesammte Staatswissenschaft*, Vol. VII (1851).

MOORE, E. C. *An Outline of the History of Christian Thought since Kant* (New York: Macmillan, 1912).

MUMFORD, LEWIS. *The Culture of Cities* (New York: Harcourt, Brace, 1938).
586 pp.

———. *Faith for Living* (New York: Harcourt, Brace, 1940). 333 pp.

NIEBUHR, REINHOLD. *The Nature and Destiny of Man* (New York: Charles
Scribner's Sons, 1941).

NIEMEYER, GERHART. *Law Without Force: The Function of Politics in International Law* (Princeton: Princeton University Press, 1941). 408 pp.

ORTEGA Y GASSET JOSÉ. *The Revolt of the Masses* (New York: Norton, 1932).
204 pp.

PARKES, H. B. *Marxism: An Autopsy* (Boston: Houghton Mifflin, 1939).
299 pp.

PFEIFER, KURT. *Die Idee der Grundrechte in der deutschen Literatur von 1790
bis Georg Jellinek (1890)* (Jena: Inaugural dissertation, 1930).

POUND, ROSCOE. *The Spirit of the Common Law* (Boston: Marshall Jones,
1921). 224 pp.

———. *Interpretations of Legal History* (New York: Macmillan, 1923).
171 pp.

PUCHTA, C. F. *Outlines of Jurisprudence as the Science of Right—A Juristic
Encyclopedia,* translated by W. Hastie (Edinburgh: 1887).

RADER, MELVIN. *No Compromise: The Conflict between Two Worlds* (New
York: Macmillan, 1939). 403 pp.

RAUSCHNING, HERMANN. *The Revolution of Nihilism: Warning to the West*
(New York: Alliance, 1939). 300 pp.

RAUSHENBUSH, STEPHEN. *The March of Fascism* (New Haven: Yale University Press, 1939). 355 pp.

READ, CONYERS (ed.). *The Constitution Reconsidered* (New York: Columbia
University Press, 1938).

ROSENBERG, ARTHUR. *Democracy and Socialism* (New York: Knopf, 1939).
369 pp.

ROUSSEAU, J. J. *The Social Contract,* translated by H. J. Tozer (3d ed.;
London: Sonnenschein, 1902). 247 pp.

RUGGIERO, GUIDO DE. *The History of European Liberalism,* translated by R. G.
Collingwood (London: Oxford University Press, 1927). 476 pp.

SABINE, G. H. *A History of Political Theory* (New York: Holt, 1937). 797 pp.

SAVIGNY, F. K. *Of the Vocation of Our Age for Legislation and Jurisprudence,* translated by A. Hayward (London: Littlewood, 1831). 182 pp.

SCHMITT, CARL. *Politische Romantik* (2d ed.; Munich: Duncker and Humblot, 1925). 234 pp.

———. *Verfassungslehre* (Munich: Duncker and Humblot, 1928). 404 pp.

———. *Der Begriff des Politischen* (3d ed.; Hamburg: Hanseatic, 1933).
61 pp.

SELIGMAN, E. R. A. *Encyclopaedia of the Social Sciences* (New York: Macmillan, 1937). 15 vols.

SHEPARD, MAX. "Sovereignty at the Crossroads," *Political Science Quarterly*
(1930). pp. 580 ff.

SMITH, ADAM. *The Theory of Moral Sentiments* (Boston: Wells and Lilly,
1817). 2 vols.

———. *Wealth of Nations,* edited by Edwin Cannan (London: Methuen, 1904). 2 vols.

SONTAG, R. J. *Germany and England: Background of Conflict 1848–1894* (New York: Appleton-Century, 1938). 362 pp.

SPANN, OTHMAR. *The History of Economics,* translated by Eden and Cedar Paul (New York: Norton, 1930). 328 pp.

SPENLÉ, JEAN-EDOUARD. *La Pensée allemande de Luther à Nietzsche* (Paris: Colin, 1934). 177 pp.

STAMMLER, RUDOLPH. *Theorie der Rechtswissenschaft* (Halle: Waisenhaus, 1911). 851 pp.

———. *Wirtschaft und Recht nach der materialistischen Geschichtsauffassung* (3d ed.; Leipzig: Veit, 1914). 704 pp.

———. "Fundamental Tendencies in Modern Jurisprudence," *Michigan Law Review,* Vol. XXI (1923), pp. 862 ff.

———. *The Theory of Justice,* translated by Isaac Husik (New York: Macmillan, 1925). 591 pp.

STEIN, LORENZ VON. *Der Begriff der Gesellschaft* (Leipzig: Wigand, 1855). 445 pp.

———. *System der Staatswissenschaft* (Stuttgart: Cotta, 1856). 2 vols.

SULLIVAN, J. W. N. *The Limitations of Science* (New York: Viking, 1933). 307 pp.

TILLICH, PAUL. *The Religious Situation,* translated by Reinhold Niebuhr (New York: Holt, 1932). 182 pp.

TRIEPEL, HEINRICH. *Völkerrecht und Landesrecht* (Leipzig: Hirschfeld, 1899). 452 pp.

WEBER, MAX. *The Protestant Ethic and the Spirit of Capitalism,* translated by Talcott Parsons (London: Allen and Unwin, 1930). 292 pp.

WHITEHEAD, A. N. *Science and the Modern World* (New York: Macmillan, 1925). 304 pp.

———. *Adventures of Ideas* (New York: Macmillan, 1933). 385 pp.

WILSON, EDMUND. *Axel's Castle: A Study of the Imaginative Literature of 1870–1930* (New York: Scribner's, 1931). 319 pp.

ZORN, PHILIPP. *Das Staatsrecht des deutschen Reiches* (Berlin: Guttentag, 1880). 460 pp.